Kelly Reichardt

Contemporary Film Directors

Edited by Justus Nieland and Jennifer Fay

The Contemporary Film Directors series provides concise, well-written introductions to directors from around the world and from every level of the film industry. Its chief aims are to broaden our awareness of important artists, to give serious critical attention to their work, and to illustrate the variety and vitality of contemporary cinema. Contributors to the series include an array of internationally respected critics and academics. Each volume contains an incisive critical commentary, an informative interview with the director, and a detailed filmography.

A list of books in the series appears at the end of this book.

Kelly Reichardt

Katherine Fusco and
Nicole Seymour

**UNIVERSITY
OF
ILLINOIS
PRESS**
URBANA,
CHICAGO,
AND
SPRINGFIELD

1 2 3 4 5 C P 5 4 3 2 1
♾ This book is printed on acid-free paper.

Frontispiece: Kelly Reichardt. Photo courtesy of David Godlis.

Library of Congress Cataloging-in-Publication Data
Names: Fusco, Katherine author. | Seymour, Nicole author.
Title: Kelly Reichardt / by Katherine Fusco and Nicole Seymour.
Description: Urbana : University of Illinois Press, 2017. | Series: Contemporary film directors | Includes bibliographical references and index. | Includes filmography. |
Identifiers: LCCN 2017020956 (print) | LCCN 2017033384 (ebook) | ISBN 9780252050107 (ebook) | ISBN 9780252041242 (hardcover : alk. paper) | ISBN 9780252083051 (pbk. : alk. paper)
Subjects: LCSH: Reichardt, Kelly—Criticism and interpretation.
Classification: LCC PN1998.3.R4325 (ebook) | LCC PN1998.3.R4325 F77 2017 (print) | DDC 791.4302/33092—dc23
LC record available at https://lccn.loc.gov/2017020956

Contents

Acknowledgments

We are grateful to the Belcourt Theater in Nashville, Tennessee, where we were lucky to see *Old Joy*, *Wendy and Lucy*, and *Meek's Cutoff* on the big screen and to lead audience discussions on Reichardt through the FLiCX (Faculty-Led interactive Cinematic eXplorations) program. Special thanks to Belcourt staff members James Cathcart and Zack Hall, FLiCX director F. Clark Williams Jr., and FLiCX program coordinator Rob Watson.

We would also like to thank the scholars who participated in our 2012 Society for Cinema and Media Studies panel on Kelly Reichardt: Matthew Holtmeier, Stephen Mitchell, Mike Phillips, and Robert Silberman.

We could not have completed this project without the help of filmscience's Anish Savjani, who helped us secure access to Reichardt's short films and early rough cuts. Our thanks as well to Jonathan Raymond and, of course, Kelly Reichardt, for making themselves available for interviews. In particular, Reichardt was generous enough to invite us into her home and allow us to meet her sweet Lucy. We also greatly appreciate the guidance and unflagging enthusiasm of series editors Jennifer Fay and Justus Nieland and acquisitions editor Daniel Nasset. In addition, we thank the anonymous reader who offered helpful feedback as we brought the project to completion.

Katherine Fusco's work on this project was supported in part by start-up funds provided by the Department of English at the University of Nevada, Reno. She also wishes to thank Kyle Weerheim for his help with images. Nicole Seymour's work on this project was supported in part by a Summer Research Fellowship from the College of Arts, Humanities, and Social Sciences Dean's Office at the University of Arkansas,

Little Rock and a Carson Fellowship from the Rachel Carson Center for Environment and Society in Munich, Germany.

Finally, this book is a true collaboration born out more than a decade of intellectual companionship and friendship. The authors are grateful for the experience of coauthoring this project.

Kelly Reichardt

Emergency and the Everyday |

Processing Emergency

Around the thirty-minute mark of *Night Moves* (2013), the fifth feature from independent U.S. filmmaker Kelly Reichardt, the protagonists build a bomb. The scene opens on the inside of a cement mixer, where fertilizer spins around and around. A cut takes us to a wider view, showing the repetitive motions of Harmon (Peter Sarsgaard) and Dena (Dakota Fanning) as they feed the mixer with a shovel and scoop the rendered explosive powder into bags with a kitchen saucepan. The next shot brings us inside the boat that will become a floating bomb once packed with these explosives—which our environmentalist protagonists will aim at a dam. Again, the focus is on painstaking labor: we watch as Josh (Jesse Eisenberg) struggles to remove the seat cushions from inside the cabin. The frame fills with the materials he has wrenched free and pushed up from the depths, blocking his face.

Though the scene centers on a series of tasks with dramatic implications, this is no montage. The infrequent cuts create long takes—the

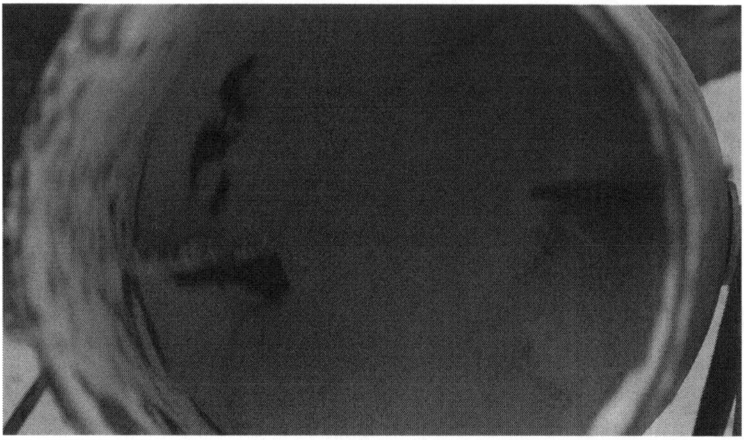

Figure 1: Mixing fertilizer in *Night Moves* |

first three average nineteen seconds each.[1] The whole scene consists of only six shots. We hear no music or dialogue, just a soundscape of work: grinding machinery, heavy breathing, and the *whomp* of plastic bags being stacked on top of each other. The transformation at hand is not a speedy one, and the deliberate pacing fails to whip us into a frenzy or ratchet up the tension.

The scene is characteristically Reichardt, right down to the inclusion of a rotating circle—here, the mouth of the cement mixer—that indicates the cycling of time. In other films, we see car, train, and wagon wheels: orbs that turn as Reichardt's characters spin further into precarious situations. In fact, it is another cement mixer that later indexes the depths of the *Night Moves* protagonists' troubles. After the bomb has detonated—offscreen, in typically unspectacular Reichardtian style—and Josh has returned to the organic farm where he works as a hired hand, he helps his coworker Surprise (Alia Shawkat) rotate fertilizer in a nearly identical contraption. This particular chore can only remind Josh, or, at least, the viewer, of the grave departure he and his compatriots have taken, destroying with the same material he currently uses to nourish. Now he kills time, waiting for his crime to catch up with him. But despite that departure, not much has changed from the earlier scene to the later: life in *Night Moves* is a series of repetitive, even circular, motions.

Figure 2: Making a bomb in *Night Moves*

These scenes exemplify Reichardt's tendency to focus on process, duration, and aftermath. In blowing up a dam, the *Night Moves* protagonists take an immediate and dramatic step. But Reichardt's film insists on the unglamorous and banal aspects of their extreme act; the chores that remain to be done, even in states of emergency. And though these protagonists are more agential than the down-and-out characters who populate the director's other features, her choice to highlight both their labor and the ultimate ineffectiveness of their attempts to jam the system that contains them is classic Reichardt. Moreover, although *Night Moves* does not explore economic decline to the degree that her other films do, a sense of decline shapes this film as well: the group's extreme act is motivated by their despair over environmental degradation.

Night Moves thus bears the trademarks of the mode that Reichardt has been developing since her 1994 debut, *River of Grass*: a slow-paced realism that highlights the precariousness of contemporary life and emphasizes the everyday, ongoing nature of emergency. Indeed, as we show in this book, two seemingly opposed concepts animate Reichardt's work to date: emergency and the everyday. Through our readings, we reframe the concept of emergency to consider its shared root with "emergence": a slow or imperceptible unfolding, especially resulting from another event or state.[2] Reichardt's spare plots and slow editing express the emergent quality of emergencies, the way that troubles quietly snowball. Following from this sense that emergencies are both slow and accumulative, we argue that living through emergency may in fact be an everyday experience. Of course, realism has long been associated with the everyday, as film history and scholarship shows. But what is notable about Reichardt's œuvre, we argue, is how it uses realism to show us that emergency, rather than constituting a *break* from the everyday, might be a version thereof.

In this way, Reichardt exposes the truth of political theorist Bonnie Honig's claim that "Emergency settings *only aggravate and accentuate the ordinary ways* in which we retrench from the more life of democracy into the mereness of mere life" (140, our emphasis). Reichardt's feature films take up what we refer to as the question of hospitality: how, in times of emergency, people treat strangers, strangers treat people, and people treat animals and landscapes. Reichardt thus asks what ethical relations might look like in emergency: Do individuals act collectively, democratically, or openly, or do they retrench? And what factors shape or constrain those choices?

Born in Miami, Florida, in 1964, Reichardt grew up with a crime-scene photographer father. It was with his camera, which he used to photograph the aftermath of crises, that Reichardt first began capturing the world around her (Haynes interview). And it was this upbringing that provided inspiration for her acclaimed first feature: set in Miami, *River of Grass* centers on the daughter of a crime-scene detective and her companion, who struggle to skip town after they think they've shot someone. Unlike that pair, Reichardt eventually escaped Florida, which she has called a "cultural wasteland" (McClanahan) for Boston, Massachusetts, where she earned a BFA from nearby Tufts University. Despite the comedic character of this early work and its personal resonances—features never seen again in the filmmaker's œuvre—*River of Grass* displays Reichardt's ongoing interest in documenting the aftermath of spectacular or isolable events.

River of Grass arrived at an auspicious time for independent film. That year, Bravo launched the Independent Film Channel, and another quirky noir, *Pulp Fiction*, burst onto the cinematic landscape, guns blazing, forever changing the picture of what independent films could achieve. On the other end of the tonal spectrum, 1994's film critics also applauded the breakout documentary hit *Hoop Dreams*. By 1997, the U.S. independent scene was sufficiently mainstream that the films competing in the Best Picture Oscar race consisted of four indies: *Shine, Fargo, The English Patient*, and *Secrets and Lies*—leading critics to dub it "The Year of the Independents."[3] Reichardt achieved great success in this climate with *River*. In addition to a Sundance Grand Jury nod, she earned three Independent Spirit Award nominations and many strong reviews. In the *Los Angeles Times*, for example, Kevin Thomas declared that "Reichardt is so agile, ingenious and funny that she can make a lively, entertaining movie about how life isn't like the movies." Even when mixed, other reviews agreed that Reichardt was one to watch.[4]

Reichardt appeared similarly optimistic in 1994, preparing for a new film that would build on *Grass*'s success and follow in its semiautobiographical vein: This second project, to be called *The Royal Court*, was to focus on a homicide detective's relationship with a widow who lost her husband to suicide, reflecting the courtship of Reichardt's father and stepmother (Haynes interview). But things began to fall apart, with Reichardt struggling to fund and retain creative control of her work. Failing to launch into the ranks of the 1990s celebrity auteurs, she would virtually disappear from the independent scene for the next twelve years.

During this period, Reichardt began living on friends' couches, taking small gigs around New York City and making shorter and nonnarrative films. These films include *Ode* (1999, 48 minutes), a narrative film loosely inspired by Bobbie Gentry's popular song "Ode to Billie Joe," about a mysterious teen suicide; *Then, a Year* (2001, 14 minutes), an experimental film consisting of suburban neighborhood images and featuring audio re-creations of elements from true-crime cases; and *Travis* (2004, 11 minutes), a nonnarrative experimental short that draws on a National Public Radio interview with the bereaved mother of an Iraq War soldier.

At the same time that Reichardt weathered professional difficulties, she saw a rightward shift in national politics—culminating in George W. Bush's election in 2000 and reelection in 2004 and overwhelming Democratic support for the Iraq War in 2003. Reichardt has described these events as devastating to her sense of U.S. political and cultural progress: "You know, the '90s was such an optimistic time. Then all the themes got so heavy. I don't know what happened! Well, I know what happened. We moved into the Bush era, and it got fucking depressing!"

(Seymour and Fusco interview). Having witnessed the Nixon impeachment hearings as a child, she found it difficult to accept that the United States would again fall in line behind a corrupt administration (Rowin). After an auspicious debut in an "optimistic time," the early 2000s thus saw Reichardt brought low by professional and political disappointments.

Two years into George W. Bush's second term, however, Reichardt reemerged with a quiet triumph. Her second feature in over a decade, *Old Joy* (2006, 76 minutes) earned glowing praise from critics; multiple award nominations and appearances on end-of-year top-ten lists; and several prizes, including a Hivos Tiger Award from the Rotterdam Film Festival and the Independent/Experimental Film and Video Award from the Los Angeles Film Critics Association. The film inaugurated her long-running collaboration with a key group of colleagues, including screenwriter Jonathan Raymond; producer (and filmmaker) Todd Haynes; producers Neil Kopp and Anish Savjani; actors James LeGros, Will Oldham, Will Patton, and Michelle Williams; and several crew members.[5] The year 2006 also saw Reichardt join a different group of colleagues, becoming a faculty member in residence at Bard College in upstate New York, where she teaches today alongside experimental filmmakers such as Peter Hutton.

Notably, *Old Joy* also inaugurated a new regional affiliation for Reichardt: the Pacific Northwest. Her first four post-*River* features have been set and filmed entirely on location in Oregon, and even her short films *Then, a Year* and *Travis* have Pacific Northwest pedigrees.[6] Raymond, Haynes, Kopp, and crew members such as location scout Roger Faires live in Oregon, and Reichardt also tends to employ actors and even nonprofessionals known for their local connections or work on films associated with the Pacific Northwest.[7] When asked by *Gothamist* magazine's Elisa Winter why she chose Oregon for the setting of *Old Joy* and *Wendy and Lucy*, Reichardt explained, "I just have a big attachment to the place . . . and my crew's out there now. But really it has to do with Jon Raymond writing for what's out[side] his window," often quite literally. One interviewer reminds Raymond of Reichardt's story of "driving all around the country trying to figure out where to shoot *Wendy and Lucy* and ending up in the parking lot [he] originally wrote about, which [he] can see from [his] house" (Adams).

Along with establishing this significant regional affiliation, Reichardt's career "reboot" entailed a notable shift in style and tone. *River of Grass* is stylized, funny, quirky, and even grotesque, descriptors that would never be applied to any of Reichardt's subsequent features. These slow, quiet, austere, and verisimilar films have earned her a reputation for bringing realist sensibilities back to U.S. independent cinema—a cinema that, since its heyday in the 1990s, has been characterized largely by the preciousness and flash of Wes Andersons and Quentin Tarantinos. This career shift, as we explain in our first section, entails a move from individually focused psychological realism to socially relevant neorealism; starting with *Old Joy*, Reichardt began a practice of tracking the unspectacular but pervasive emergencies common to many, not just the quirky few.

These practices have prompted critics to identify Reichardt as both a "neo-neo realist" and a figurehead of "slow cinema."[8] We agree with these categorical appraisals but see room to parse them more carefully and explore their implications more critically. For example, we note that, while Reichardt's post-*River* films bring European neorealism to bear on postindustrial U.S. issues, she rejects the sentimentality often associated with filmmakers such as Vittorio De Sica. She also declines to ask audiences to care about or identify with particular characters; instead, she asks that we consider the structural limitations placed on them. We also show how even some of those critics and scholars who appreciate Reichardt's slow cinema misconstrue it, seeing her films' slowness as a respite from busy modern life rather than a way to capture the negative modern realities of decline and degradation.

With a story by Jesse Hartman and Reichardt and a screenplay by Reichardt, *River of Grass* offers a send-up of the lovers-on-the-run plot so popular in the 1990s. Dissatisfied housewife Cozy (Lisa Bowman) abandons her family and takes up with Lee (Larry Fessenden), a ne'er-do-well who just happens to be in possession of the gun that Cozy's detective father has lost. The gun goes off, and the pair, mistakenly believing they have killed someone, go on the lam. Living in a fleabag motel and committing petty crimes to survive, they never succeed in escaping their local area.

Old Joy adapts Raymond's short story of the same name, which centers on two men attempting to recapture a fading friendship on a brief camping trip in the Oregon forest. Trained on the interactions between the flaky, itinerant Kurt (prolific musician and occasional actor Oldham) and the stable, middle-class Mark (Daniel London), the film explodes transcendentalist notions of finding oneself in the wilderness. As the pair fall into increasingly strained conversations about their respective life choices and contributions to society, Kurt and Mark lose their literal and metaphorical way—and their sense of whatever once bonded them together.

Reichardt's next film, *Wendy and Lucy* (2008), was coscripted with Raymond.[9] The film traces how an automobile breakdown transforms a young, lower-middle-class white woman into a de facto drifter. Drawn by the old promise of riches out West, hoping to make good with a job in an Alaskan cannery, Wendy from Indiana (Williams) instead finds herself stranded in small-town Oregon, struggling to support herself and her dog Lucy. The film again garnered Reichardt multiple honors, including a nomination for the *Un Certain Regard* award at the Cannes Film Festival.

Reichardt moved from Wendy's western quest to an actual western—though a revisionist one—with *Meek's Cutoff* (2010), featuring an original screenplay by Raymond inspired by the journals of women on the Oregon Trail. The only one of Reichardt's features not set in the contemporary moment, the film records the experience of Manifest Destiny as one of terrifying uncertainty. Having lost their way, their faith in their guide Stephen Meek (Bruce Greenwood), and much of their water supply, Reichardt's travelers (Paul Dano, Shirley Henderson, Neal Huff, Zoe Kazan, Tommy Nelson, Patton, and Williams) encounter a Native American man (Rod Rondeaux) who may be their salvation or yet another threat to their survival. *Meek's* once again received multiple nominations and honors, including an Independent Spirit Award for producer Anish Savjani.

Reichardt's most recent Oregon film, with an original screenplay cowritten with Raymond, was less critically acclaimed than its three predecessors but nonetheless received honors such as a nomination for the Golden Lion Award at the Venice Film Festival. *Night Moves* brings the filmmaker's underlying interests in environmental issues to the fore while maintaining her interest in aftermath scenarios. After the conspirators

Dena, Harmon, and Josh accidentally kill a camper in the execution of their plot, the toll of their actions weighs on them until a paranoid Josh murders Dena. He winds up alone, on the run, and without money or resources at the film's end. As the cement mixer scenes portend, little changes as a result of the group's actions: the dams and development remain pervasive, overwhelming forces, and the remaining conspirators are as alienated and disenfranchised as ever, if not more so.

As we were completing this manuscript, Reichardt's most recent film, *Certain Women* (2016), went into limited theatrical release after a successful festival run, garnering a Best Film award from the London Film Festival and a Best Supporting Actress award for Lily Gladstone from the Los Angeles Film Critics Association. Though we do not treat the film in depth in this book, several points are worth establishing here. First, *Certain Women* marks Reichardt's move to a new geographical locale—bleak, small-town Montana—and new source material—Maile Meloy's 2009 short-story collection, *Both Ways Is the Only Way I Want It*. It also marks the first time since *River of Grass* that a Reichardt film has featured more than one plot. The first part of the film covers the relationship between a lawyer (Laura Dern) and a client (Jared Harris) who has been left disabled and disenfranchised by his employers after a construction-site accident; the second depicts a woman's (Michelle Williams) negotiations over materials for a house that her cheating husband (James LeGros) has promised to build for her; and the third details the failed attempts of a lonely ranchhand (Gladstone) to form a connection with a visiting night-school teacher (Kristen Stewart). Though we come to understand that these three sets of characters are loosely connected to one another, we never see more than the most glancing of interactions between them. Moreover, Reichardt eschews crosscutting, presenting the stories sequentially. She thus maintains her trademark slow-paced realism and intense focus on the everyday.

As these synopses hint, Reichardt's career to date is concerned with various types of U.S. failures. It also is concerned with two particular types of emergencies: environmental degradation and economic decline. We see her as one of very few filmmakers looking at the two together—not as separate concerns and not, as political discourse often has it, as opposing concerns. In our work, then, we both draw on and draw together recent scholarship on these respective emergencies. For example, ecocritic and postcolonial scholar Rob Nixon has brought attention to environmental crises such as oil spills and climate change as "violence of delayed destruction that is dispersed across time and space . . . violence that is typically not viewed as violence at all" (2); we identify the slow cinema movement with which Reichardt is associated as a means of capturing what Nixon calls "slow violence" (2). On the question of the economic, meanwhile, queer and cultural theorist Lauren Berlant has theorized our present neoliberal moment as one characterized by a perverse mass investment in a fraying set of Western postwar fantasies such as "upward mobility, job security, political and social equality . . . meritocracy, the sense that liberal-capitalist society will reliably provide opportunities for individuals to carve out relations of reciprocity that seem fair and that foster life as a project of adding up to something and constructing cushions for enjoyment" (3)—a "cruel optimism," as Berlant terms it, that "has developed belatedly" as these fantasies hold "less and less traction" and persist even and perhaps especially in the face of economic decline (3). We find, in Reichardt's films, that characters are stricken with a similar optimism in the face of a particularly U.S. postindustrial downward mobility.

We therefore see Reichardt's body of work as exemplary of what Berlant (who does not mention our filmmaker) calls "the cinema of precarity, in which attention to a pervasive contemporary social precariousness marks a relation to [both] older traditions of neorealism . . . [and] new aesthetic forms" (7). This cinema registers the current "structural pressures of crisis and loss that are wearing out the power of the good life's traditional fantasy bribe without wearing out the need for a good life" (7). But we insist that "crisis and loss," for Reichardt, includes the environmental and not just the economic. The term *precarity* helps explain both Reichardt's narrative pacing and tone throughout her filmography, as she develops a sense of dread without necessarily arriving at a culminating event. Her films thus render the *experience* of precarity, not just its plain facts or architects—as do flashier, faster films such as *Wall Street: Money Never Sleeps* (dir. Oliver Stone, 2010), *Margin Call* (dir. J. C. Chandor, 2011), and the recent Oscar nominee *The Big Short* (dir. Adam McKay, 2015). We also should note that all of Reichardt's characters can be read as part of the socioeconomic class, born of contemporary neoliberalism and intensified by factors like the

Great Recession, attendant austerity measures, and the rise of the freelance and contractor economies, that has been dubbed "the precariat." As British economist Guy Standing explains, "The precariat [is] not part of the 'working class' or the 'proletariat.' The latter terms suggest a society consisting mostly of workers in long-term, stable, fixed-hour jobs with established routes of advancement, subject to unionisation and collective agreements, with job titles their fathers and mothers would have understood, facing local employers whose names and features they were familiar with" (6). In this sense, Reichardt's variety of neorealism is historically unique; whereas midcentury neorealists focused on the already desperately poor or lower working classes, her features center on people who are slowly going downhill socioeconomically—or whom we can easily imagine doing so.

Environmental degradation and economic decline are both crises of duration: though they may have memorable flashpoints, they are long in the making and slow to unfold, and they have far-reaching consequences. And they both have in common the problem of representation, characterized as they are by their abstractness, their complexity, their multiplicity of causes and effects, and their massiveness of geographical and temporal scale. These features make the emergencies of environmental degradation and economic decline difficult to recognize *as emergencies*. And these features make them unspectacular and, thus, uncinematic—unsuited, that is, to typical feature filmmaking. And yet, it is to the representation of these emergencies that Reichardt has devoted her career.

In each of our following five sections, we focus on a major aspect of Reichardt's engagement with emergency and the everyday: her realist style, her concern with precarity, her engagement with duration, her interest in environment, and her focus on aftermath. Each of these sections centers on one or two of her feature films, with the exception of the last—in which we treat multiple works from her œuvre, including her short films.

Shifting Realisms: *River of Grass* to *Old Joy*

With more than a decade between them, Reichardt's first two feature films could easily be mistaken as the works of two different directors.[10]

While 1994's *River of Grass* is a coolly ironic spin on a crime caper, 2006's *Old Joy* trains a quiet focus on two friends on a hike. Despite the obvious differences at the level of plot and style, however, the two films share a skepticism toward mainstream filmmaking practices that is characteristically Reichardt. In both films, Reichardt experiments with realism's capacity for portraying everyday lives, although hers is an invocation of realism that has transformed over time. In *River of Grass*, Reichardt works in the tradition of psychological realism to explore the life of a misfit, and her later films shift away from interiority and update neorealism in a radically unsentimental manner in order to expose the pervasive crises of the new millennium. At stake in Reichardt's shifting realism is the matter of individualism, which comes under scrutiny in her later films, as they refuse to make the political personal; Reichardt's post-*River* realism eschews neoliberalism's emphasis on personal responsibility, choice, and freedom. By moving away from a realism more interested in psychology toward neorealism, which emphasizes situation and unravels causal relations among plot events, Reichardt departs from what David Ingram describes as Hollywood's tendency "to formulate social and political problems as conflicts between *individuals*" (4, our emphasis). Emphasizing characters' experiences, rather than their motivations, and shifting focus from individual choice onto the situational, Reichardt undercuts the pervasive tendency for audiences to ask of characters living in emergency states, "How did they get here? Why didn't they do X or Y?" Finally, we suggest that Reichardt's depersonalizing neo-neorealism allows her films to stand as a criticism of contemporary liberals who respond to structural and pervasive emergencies by focusing on their individual choices and political self-expression. In other words, although *Old Joy*'s Mark and Kurt may see themselves as masters of their own destinies, as we shall see, Reichardt's realism cuts against such individualist stances in order to reveal emergency as an organizing structure of contemporary life.

Set in Dade County, Florida, *River of Grass* tells the story of a dissatisfied housewife named Cozy who falls in with an unemployed young man named Lee. Though Cozy doesn't know it, Lee happens to have in his possession the very same gun that Cozy's police-officer father Jimmy Ryder has lost. Together, Lee and Cozy break into a backyard swimming pool, and, when the owner comes into the yard to investigate, the gun accidentally fires, leading Cozy and Lee to assume they have killed the man. They lay low for a while and then try (and fail) to cross the county border by car. The film features the same misfits-on-the-lam plot seen in many post–*Bonnie and Clyde* (dir. Arthur Penn, 1967) texts, and in many films contemporaneous with its 1994 release, such as David Lynch's *Wild at Heart* (1990), Ridley Scott's *Thelma and Louise* (1991), Greg Araki's *The Living End* (1992), Dominic Sena's *Kalifornia* (1993), and Oliver Stone's *Natural Born Killers* (1994). But while technically on the lam, Cozy and Lee never really *go* on the lam: after having supposedly committed murder, the pair stay in their hometown area, living in a fleabag motel and reflecting on their actions. They even return to Lee's house at one point to steal records from his mother. When Cozy and Lee finally screw up the courage to leave the Miami area, a police officer forces them to turn around because they cannot pay the twenty-five-cent toll. Finally, Cozy shoots Lee and pushes him out of the car. Cozy's childlike voiceover overlies the series of misbegotten events, attempting to paint the pair's pathetic criminality in grandiose romantic terms. Ironically, the narration ends just before Cozy commits a real crime, murder, as though exhausted by keeping up the lie. As Nick Salvato has described the protagonists, "they fail to achieve the level of arousal to engage in their promised affair" (17). Such ironizing of road movie tropes was in fact part of the film's publicity campaign from the start: the DVD cover features the tagline "Being outlaws was rougher than they thought," and the poster promises "A girl, a gun, and nowhere to go."[11]

The film's place among other 1990s crime films makes *River of Grass* seem very far from the realism for which Reichardt would later become known. But a conversation with her friend Todd Haynes reveals a continuity in Reichardt's films as well as an early interest in realism. Haynes observes, "There's this cool, ironic, and elegant style which pervades *River of Grass*. It's not a realistic movie. Is this something you think about—style versus realism? Is the whole idea of truth in movies something that motivates you?" Reichardt's response reveals her idiosyncratic thinking around realism:

> I do like realism in the movies—just not to the point where you aren't sure why you're at the movies. But my favorite films are about regular guys with big

> obsessions over regular things. Like the song-sheet salesman [Arthur, played by Steve Martin] in Dennis Potter's *Pennies From Heaven* [1981; written by Potter but directed by Herbert Ross]—he's killing himself trying to open a record store. You think the record store is his ultimate dream except every time a record plays, he gets lost in a fantasy where he's actually leading the band. So opening a record store is just to give him easier access to his ultimate fantasy. As it is, his wife is giving him grief for just wanting his own record store. I'm not sure why I'm off on Dennis Potter when we're talking about realism.

A realism that makes audiences unsure "why [they're] at the movies" will be the basis of many negative critiques of Reichardt's later style. But this is not the style of either *River of Grass* or *Pennies from Heaven*. Instead, *River of Grass* contains a number of self-conscious stylistic flourishes. Perhaps most obviously, Reichardt deploys the highly artificial convention of black intertitles that mark time into "chapters"—a distinct difference from her later works' more fluid experience of temporality and from their general lack of showiness and self-consciousness. A stark white bullet hole decorates each of these chapter announcements—an ironic image in a film characterized not by shootouts or spectacular violence but, instead, by a longing for such significant events. Specifically, *River of Grass* engages with a kind of psychological realism at the same time that it deflates the fantasies of both its protagonist and the action-cinema narratives about which she fantasizes. In distinguishing among realist appeals, David Bordwell has suggested that art cinema may be "a cinema of psychological effects in search of their causes" ("Art Cinema," 718). Bordwell's invocation of stylized, experimental art cinema films such as *Hiroshima Mon Amour* (dir. Alain Resnais, 1959) and *Jules et Jim* (dir. François Truffaut, 1962) in his discussion reminds us that films engaged in psychological realism may not strive for realism in other categories, such as the visual, the narrative, or the ontological. On the one hand, Bordwell's account of psychological realism—as opposed to stylistic or social realism—helps explicate Reichardt's project in *River of Grass*, as well as its difference from her later works. On the other, Reichardt's interest in "regular guys with big obsessions" suggests the beginning of her abiding commitment to chronicling U.S. failure, here filtered through Cozy's strange psyche.

River of Grass achieves its psychological realism through two related techniques: first-person voiceover narration and use of backstory, which is conveyed primarily through the narration. Traditionally, voiceover narration gives a protagonist interiority and solidifies the audience's sense of her as an individual with motivations, hopes, and dreams. Notably, *River of Grass* is the only Reichardt feature to employ this technique.[12] *River of Grass* also is unique among Reichardt's works in that it offers backstory; Reichardt's later films offer very little information about their protagonists, thus calling audiences to engage primarily with the situation at hand—often, immediate and universally human needs such as shelter, food, transportation, and water—and to imagine the protagonists as representative figures.[13] Instead, Cozy's narration and backstory make *River of Grass* fundamentally her story. As she reflects on a childhood with a hard-drinking mother and entertains romantic notions ("I wondered if there was any other person on this planet as lonely as me. It turned out there was, and he [Lee] lived just a county away"), a sense of a woman on the edge emerges. But, as Bordwell notes of psychological realism, *River of Grass* doesn't extend its "analysis at the level of groups or institutions" ("Art Cinema," 719). Instead, it immerses viewers in one woman's fantasy life. Thus, while the desperate Cozy shares with Wendy of *Wendy and*

Figure 3: Cozy at home in *River of Grass* |

Lucy and Emily of *Meek's Cutoff* a dream of a better life, the film's narration keeps audiences closer to her fantasy world, whereas Reichardt's later films distance us from the characters' personal motivations.

Considering *River of Grass* in the context of psychological realism, Reichardt's seemingly inappropriate invocation of *Pennies from Heaven* makes sense. But the reference also suggests the potential limitations of these absurdist, stylized films for political critique. In Ross's film, the strange comedic flourishes and song-and-dance numbers in dream sequences insulate audiences from Arthur's disturbing actions—including humiliating his wife (Jessica Harper) for her sexual frigidity and seducing and then abandoning a woman (Bernadette Peters) to a life of prostitution. Similarly focused on a character's inner fantasy life, the sometimes gruesome realities depicted by *River of Grass* are undercut by preposterousness. The film opens by invoking a long history of domestic violence: Cozy and her husband's home is an old crime scene, a house bought at auction after a woman killed her husband and sealed him in its walls. Further, Cozy's neglect of her children—leaving an infant sprawled on the couch when she leaves the house, for example—and her wish for a "couple in a big station wagon to come and take these kids away" may reflect the real-world desperation of mothers such as Susan Smith, the U.S. woman who sought freedom via multiple infanticide the same year *River of Grass* appeared in theaters. But although Cozy's dissatisfaction with motherhood and a domestic life lived on the edge of poverty may be "realistic," the film veers into the quirky grotesquery found in the works of indie *enfants terribles* such as Harmonie Korine and Todd Solondz: witness Cozy pouring Coca-Cola into a baby bottle for her child or turning clumsy cartwheels in front of her tract home while her children scream from their playpen. Costuming and staging compound the unreality of Reichardt's tract-home grotesqueness: costumer Sarah Jane Slotnick puts Cozy in unflattering stretch pants, and Reichardt's framing of a scene in which Cozy performs acrobatic routines in a straight-on shot of a wood-paneled living room adds a stylized performative aspect to the scene. Later in the film, when Lee robs a convenience store, he inexplicably steals a cheap wig, which Cozy wears for the film's remainder. The characters' idiosyncrasies thus draw focus from the larger structural issues at play.[14] Their alienating strangeness, and not their social class, emerges from such images.[15] *River of Grass* portrays a woman who has made a series of bad and sometimes unreasonable choices. And though other Reichardt characters will go on to choose badly, their comparative inscrutability and underindividualization means that their reasons, both psychological and biographical, can play no role in audiences' estimations of them. In *River of Grass*, whatever emergency situation Cozy finds herself in, the film does little to suggest that it is anything but a disaster of her own making.

The film processes the broader world of Miami in a correspondingly idiosyncratic manner. From the 1980s through the early 1990s, Dade County witnessed high racial tensions, a devastating hurricane, severe economic difficulties, and the violent, often drug-related crime wave memorialized in pop culture texts such as *Miami Vice*. But although Reichardt's film makes this historical context relatively plain, it offers no incisive commentary. Indeed, it regularly offers desperation as comedy. For example, when Cozy's crime-scene-specialist father visits apartments where humans have met violent ends, he rescues their now-orphaned pets; a humorous scene shows him washing the blood off a hamster. And when Reichardt gives her audience an uncomfortable encounter with documentary realism, the occasion is similarly comic. The police chief's trophy wife comes into the station, done up in a garish, lime-green-sequined dress, and peers at crime-scene photos in the break room that show bloody, half-clothed male bodies dumped on the roadside (possible victims of the drug war?). It is interesting that Reichardt presents these photos as a series of still insert shots, isolated through a presentational rather than point-of-view perspective—as if acknowledging that they do not fit into the film's seriocomic world.[16]

Much of the film's comedic tone emerges from the interplay between its formal techniques and the hapless lives of its characters, undercutting the romance of the road movie in which Cozy and Lee fancy themselves as leads. It does so most prominently through the mismatch between Cozy's voiceover and what appears on screen. At one point Cozy asks, "Do you ever wonder what it would be like to be holed up in some motel somewhere, seeing your life played out on TV, knowing that the whole world was lookin for ya?" But this rumination is placed over a shot of a motel with cars driving past, then a shot of Cozy lying on the bed. Reichardt's images here play against Cozy's statements—the television is *not* on, and there's no indication that what she's describing is actually happening. Apparently, Cozy doesn't know what it's like to be holed up under the conditions she describes, either. The film abounds with such ironic moments. For instance, when Cozy remarks in a voiceover, "I didn't know much about holdups, and Lee didn't want me getting in the way of his crime spree," what we see on the screen is Lee entering a laundromat and coming out with someone else's clothes. Throughout the film, Cozy renders their spree in glamorous terms, but Reichardt shows again and again the insignificance of their exploits. Cozy commits herself to a crime spree because popular culture teaches that such narratives have excitement and meaningful shape—only to find that she can't succeed even at being a criminal. And the many scenes of Cozy and Lee hiding out at a motor court motel show that being wanted by the law is rather boring. Cozy wanders out of their room to get a Coke in order to have something to do, not because she is thirsty; she and Lee lay languidly in the hotel bed, passing a joint back and forth between their toes to add a challenge to their otherwise dull waiting game. In his work on *River of Grass*, Salvato has suggested that Reichardt's filmmaking offers "a conceptual model for thinking about the transition from laziness to slowness, one in which spending time must give way to the fraught effort of saving it" (17). Though Cozy clearly exemplifies the former, her inability to extract herself from her bad situation shows how thin the line is between spending time badly and losing control over how one's time is spent. Though Cozy's motivating desire to live out a romantic, criminal existence is more countercultural than the economic hopes driving Reichardt's more typical protagonists, she nonetheless joins their ranks as an unsuccessful dreamer. As such, she marks the first entry in Reichardt's menagerie of U.S. failures.

But while the ironic contrast between Cozy's eventful voiceover and the unspectacular events on screen suggest Reichardt's interest in deflating traditional Hollywood narratives, the plot's emphasis on the magical coincidence rather than the random accident distinguishes this film from her later neo-neorealist narratives. With characters who unintentionally, almost stupidly, come together (it's Cozy's high school teacher whose swimming pool the duo invades), the editing and plotting in *River of Grass* offers less of what Bordwell describes as the "drifting" quality of realist narration, in which "events may lead to nothing" ("Art Cinema," 718); instead, though *River of Grass*'s characters are generally hapless, the film's editing and plotting portray them as nonetheless producing a series of events that shape the overall outcome of the film story. The film sets this up from the beginning: A few scenes after Jimmy Ryder loses his gun, we see Lee standing in front of a wall covered in a large alligator graffito, talking with a friend who has discovered Ryder's weapon. A scene later, the friend gives Lee the gun to sell. When Jimmy's daughter Cozy goes out to a bar, it happens to be Lee that she meets. And at the end of the film, when Cozy dumps the gun, she happens to be driving by the very same wall with the painted alligator. On the one hand, the circularity of the lost gun subplot may underscore the trapped quality of the characters' lives—something Reichardt's later protagonists will share. But taken together, Fessenden's editing and the just-so coincidences of the plot support, rather than undermine, Cozy's romantic belief in fate. In one of the more interestingly edited moments of *River of Grass*, the sound of Jimmy's drums plays over a variety of scenes, stitching together several separate plotlines—Jimmy playing music, Lee getting a tattoo, Cozy showering and then putting on sexy underwear. The running beat of the drums suggests the simultaneity and connectedness of all the characters, who will indeed collide, setting off the film's plot events. The film's emphasis on coincidence renders all relations individual or magical, rather than historical or structural. In contrast, as we discuss later, in work in which Reichardt moves on to neorealism, she will focus on accidents, not coincidences—a distinction important to showing the way small and random events may nonetheless derail a life.

Tellingly, the film ends with Cozy stuck in traffic, just as she is trapped in her bad marriage and trapped in Dade County. Such moments reveal traces of the sensibilities that define Reichardt's later features, as we see in *River of Grass*'s alternate ending, included in the DVD extras. What we see at the conclusion of the theatrical release is the following sequence of events: Lee tells Cozy that his friend and the friend's girlfriend have a "pretty cheap" apartment, and, in a burst of optimism not unlike that which we will see with our protagonist in *Wendy and Lucy*, he fantasizes, "We can stay with them. I can get a job, maybe get two jobs for a while, get some money coming in . . . couple months we can get an apartment, maybe in the same complex." Cozy interrupts this speech by shooting Lee and pushing him out of the car, rejecting a return to the domesticity she has been fleeing since they met. The film ends with Cozy driving away. But the alternate ending continues beyond this point. Outtakes show Lee still alive, lying and breathing at the side of the road after Cozy has shot him and driven away. He then gets up and starts to walk. Such an outcome is funnier than anything we have seen from Reichardt since. But this alternate version of the film still presages the type of dramatic irony and genre play Reichardt would develop in her later, more serious works. In addition to allowing audiences to know something the protagonist doesn't (Lee survives, unbeknownst to Cozy, just as other Reichardt characters don't know things that audience members do), an ironic relation to typical Hollywood plotting emerges. Even the most spectacular actions—abruptly shooting someone and pushing him out of a moving car—are contained within a broader circularity that diffuses them. As in Reichardt's later films, this first feature ends with the protagonist stuck, her dream unachieved, her future uncertain.

Among its other distinguishing features, *River of Grass* is the only feature film that Reichardt did not edit herself; in addition to playing Lee, Larry Fessenden served as editor.[17] But during her twelve-year break from feature filmmaking after *River*, Reichardt made the short film *Then, a Year*, which she cited in our interview with her as an important exercise in learning to edit. We would suggest that the development of this technique is crucial in understanding Reichardt's shift away from psychological realism. Her later neo-neorealism emerges in large part from editing techniques that allow the environments in which her characters find themselves to become central, including long takes, minimal crosscutting, and "post-action lag" (Singer 59), shots that linger after characters have left the frame.[18] Short film also allowed Reichardt to explore new thematic and formal ground—again, sowing seeds for her later, more classically-realist features. Although she had originally planned to follow *River of Grass* with a tale inspired by personal tragedy (see the Introduction's discussion of the aborted project *The Royal Court*), the three short films she made during her break explore other people's tragedies: 1999's *Ode* details a queer youth's suicide in a small Southern town through an extended flashback; 2001's nonnarrative visual pastiche *Then, a Year* explores the fallout of sensational crimes; and 2004's *Travis* conveys the lasting grief of a soldier's bereaved mother. Reichardt has carried these tendencies forward in her subsequent features, departing from idiosyncratic, individualized characters in favor of more representative ones.

In addition to these focal shifts, Reichardt also made a shift in production style in her return to feature filmmaking. She has reflected on *River of Grass* as her one experiment working with big crews—a process she disliked, and which led to her disillusionment with the politics and practices of large-scale feature filmmaking (Van Sant interview). On set, Reichardt experienced the sexism that exists even in the indie world:

> I had written this script, lived with it and raised the money, yet I still had to go to the set each day and defend my post as director. It was the first time in my life that I was like, Oh, I get it, this is happening because I'm a five-foot-tall female—I wasn't given the benefit of the doubt from a lot of the men and women on my shoot. I fought for every shot in my film, which is such a drain and something I wasn't prepared for. (Haynes interview)[19]

Whereas *River of Grass* pursued multiple storylines in multiple locations, when it came to *Old Joy*, Reichardt only wanted to and only could afford to make a film with a stripped-down story. Discussing the difference between shooting *Old Joy* and her first feature, Reichardt explains, "There was an intimacy to the way the film [*Old Joy*] was made—a sped up intimacy. . . . I would never want a crew of 13 again, as on *River of Grass*. I don't [even] want a crew of 10. I just want to make a film where there are no walkie-talkies or Blackberries. . . . [W]hich means I won't have a dolly shot, but that's okay" (Rowin). In other interviews, Reichardt explicitly emphasizes the financial costs of filmmaking (a consideration that also influenced the styles of neorealism, a movement most associated with filmmakers coming from an economically decimated post–World War II Italy). In describing her decision to make *Old Joy*, Reichardt explains how she came to choose a Jon Raymond short story as her next project: "I was trying to think about what I could actually afford to make, and I was talking about short stories that happen mostly outside, trying to think about something I could do in a slightly bigger way than *Ode*. But not too much—just available light and a minimal amount of characters" (Rowin).[20] In her work on Reichardt, Elena Gorfinkel associates this stripped down style with global austerity movements:

> Austerity, a loaded term, resonates with a twenty-first century economic order and the neoliberal imperatives and policies of the George W. Bush and

post-Bush era that insist that citizens do less with less, policies of resource attrition that have led to the dispossession of the already marginalized. In that sense, Reichardt's austere slowness is an aesthetic responsive to the harsh economic and ideological realities of the United States's political contemporaneity. ("Exhausted Drift," 124)

As with the neorealists before her, then, the practical economic realities of Reichardt's filmmaking shape her features.

The classic neorealist feature film, as exemplified by works such as *Ladri di biciclette* (*The Bicycle Thieves*, Vittorio De Sica, 1948) and *Umberto D.* (De Sica, 1952), is characterized by a tendency toward some or all of the following elements: long takes; long shots; deep focus; a lack of flashbacks or flash-forwards; simple plots; loose causality; an episodic quality; circumscribed geography and temporality; a focus on everyday people, especially the poor and otherwise down-and-out; the use of nonprofessional actors; and on-location shooting.[21] Neorealism's greatest champion, André Bazin, understood the movement as a "useful and intelligent reaction against the Italian aesthetic of the super-spectacle and, for that matter, more generally, against the technical aestheticism from which the cinema suffered all over the world" ("Bicycle Thieves," 61). For Bazin, technical aestheticism seals off the artwork from political concerns, and, in the context of post–World War II era Italian film, we might also understand the simplicity, smallness, and grittiness of neorealism as an important rejection of entertainments that did not address the suffering of everyday people.

Although Reichardt's post–*River of Grass* filmmaking favors most of the classic neorealist elements just enumerated, it responds to different political and economic realities—including neoliberalism, postindustrialism, globalization, economic downturn or the so-called "Great Recession," environmental degradation, and their associated phenomena, including downward mobility and the rise of the precariat. Repurposing post–World War II techniques for the twenty-first century, Reichardt's features from *Old Joy* onward reflect on a neoliberalism that offers no structures of care for the vulnerable and instead shifts responsibility to individuals and the market. But with the exception of her fifth feature, the explicitly political *Night Moves*, Reichardt's work exemplifies Bazin's concept of neorealism as implicitly political cinema. Describing De Sica's *Ladri di biciclette*, Bazin explains that the "social message is not detached; it remains immanent in the event, but it is so clear that nobody can overlook it, still less take exception to it, since it is never made explicitly a message" ("Bicycle Thieves," 65). That is to say, Reichardt's neo-neorealist films are generally not directly political in theme. Instead, they depict the everyday lives of characters who are caught up nonetheless in situations with deep political and economic resonance. For example, in films such as *Old Joy* and *Wendy and Lucy*, Reichardt shoots from car windows, or tracks alongside walking characters, to reveal what has happened to both labor and landscape in the postindustrial present-day Pacific Northwest.

In addition to deploying neorealism's on-location shooting, long shots, and long takes to reveal economic and environmental decline, Reichardt also uses neorealism's spare narrative style to scale ideas of global emergency down to the size of lived, everyday experience. Despite using individual characters to make the costs of contemporary emergencies apparent, however, Reichardt refuses to treat her characters sentimentally or melodramatically. In fact, although the Italian neorealists were sometimes criticized for their "facile sentimentality" (Bazin, "De Sica," 78), Reichardt updates neorealism with a relentless antisentimentality, retaining its "revolutionary humanism" (Bazin, "Cinematic Realism," 33) even as she alienates viewers from her characters through a focus on either unlikable or opaque protagonists. By making her characters less lovable than their neorealist predecessors, Reichardt draws attention to contemporary society's unwillingness to care for those with whom it may be difficult to identify. Reichardt also utilizes new visual strategies to underpin her exploration of the U.S. precariat, most notably postaction lag. This is a decidedly antisentimental technique; her camera acts as if it doesn't care enough about its human or animal protagonists to follow them out of frame, thereby mimicking the way a society may be happy enough to let its "failures" drift from view.

In *Old Joy*, her earliest Oregon film, Reichardt clarifies how neoliberalism's emphasis on individualism, the free-market global economy, and the privatization of care creates conditions of emergency for some at the same time that it creates conditions of success for others. She does so through her neorealist visual style, which emphasizes the environment in which her characters exist. Furthermore, through dialogue and plot, she reveals the way in which an emphasis on individual expression, associated with both the New Left and contemporary leftists, distracts from underlying economic structures. In contrast to *River of Grass*, the plot of *Old Joy* is spare, following in the tradition of neorealism: The film features two friends who have not seen each other for a number of years getting together for a camping and hiking trip at Bagby Hot Springs. Kurt (Will Oldham) has retained the countercultural attitude of his youth and is living an existence on the fringe of society, while Mark (Daniel London) appears to have achieved a more middle-class existence. Mark seems to judge Kurt for not "growing up," at the same time that Kurt judges him for abandoning a more alternative lifestyle. Reichardt has stated that the film's title may be understood as a reference to her generation's political sense: "People my age have the feeling now that any kind of idealism, that any kind of justice would prevail, has been shot to hell. That's the old joy of it. These guys [protagonists Mark and Kurt] not being able to be effectual. . . . *Old Joy* has a feeling of my generation at a total loss" (Rowin). Though Reichardt here discusses liberals' political inefficacy as a *fait accompli*, the film offers a meditation on *how* efficacy is lost, an emphasis on the processes and attitudes that make up the failure of today's leftists.

Reichardt does so by giving us protagonists who present cultivation of the self as political engagement, albeit in different ways: Kurt is grasping at the alternative and itinerant lifestyle of his twenties, seemingly to his detriment, and Mark has settled into a nice bourgeois life replete with comfortable home, Volvo, and pregnant wife. But if Mark embodies the modern-day mildly engaged condition of contemporary bourgeois liberals, Reichardt is sympathetic to this position, even as the film expresses a concern with his mode of political engagement. In an interview, Reichardt explains that Mark's condition is easy to slip into: "I can relate to those guys—I definitely sit in my apartment and listen to too much Air America [the short-lived progressive talk radio channel]. It's so easy to feel very righteous. . . . You feel like you've done something without doing anything at all but walk around your house going, 'Right on!'" (Rowin). In her portrayal of Mark, Reichardt reveals this state of righteousness to be no less isolating, no less insufficient, than Kurt's. Whereas Kurt will alienate those around him over the course of the film, Reichardt shows Mark continuously turning inward in the name of good leftist behavior. Indeed, the film opens with Mark meditating outside, eyes closed, engaging in sensory withdrawal from the world around him. A different kind of withdrawal inheres in Mark's primary habit in the film: driving around, listening to the radio—Air America, of course—with his gaze straight ahead, not engaging with the world outside his window. Much like his meditation garden, his car becomes a sanctuary and the radio an insulating soundtrack. Whether exploring Kurt's countercultural commitments, or Mark's impotent political posturing, Reichardt's neo-neorealism casts the men's investments in their self-expression against an environmentally and economically deteriorating environment, thereby revealing the way even today's leftists have bought into the ideology of individuality that has supported the emergency that is neoliberalism.

Yet another of Reichardt's realist references clarifies the stakes of her neo-neorealist approach. Admitting that "I know I'm not capable of making an out-and-out political film," Reichardt told interviewer Michael Joshua Rowin that she nonetheless "saw in the characters' relationship a metaphor: two lost liberals trying to find their way. . . . As much as I thought about a film like *Shampoo*, I know *Old Joy* is not *Shampoo*." Indeed, Reichardt's film appears quite unlike Hal Ashby's 1975 satire; its intimate sadness operates on a different emotional scale than that sneering look at Los Angeles. But as with the inspiration *River of Grass* took from *Pennies from Heaven*, the connection Reichardt draws here is telling.[22] Like Ashby's promiscuous hairdresser and his clients, who bed-hop and light up obliviously as time races toward Nixon's game-changing election, Mark and Kurt also are distracted by the outward trappings of their liberal politics. In Ashby's film, the hairdresser George (Warren Beatty) and his various client-lovers have no explicit political commitments; rather, they *feel* an affinity for the Beatles-listening, joint-smoking hippies whose party they crash at the end of the film after attending a pro-Nixon election party earlier that night. As the appearance of a square conservative financier at the party demonstrates, if all it means to be part of the counterculture is to smoke marijuana and get into a hot tub with other naked people (a scene Reichardt winks at in both *Old Joy* and *Night Moves*, which contain much more ominous hot-springs–tub interactions), then anyone can co-opt the spirit of liberals—even the twentieth century's ultimate square, Richard Nixon, who appears at the end of *Shampoo* via a television set, insisting he wants to reunite the country by joining together with young people.

Though the hippies of Ashby's film do not show up in *Old Joy*, we might imagine Mark and Kurt as their children, two figures who have been too busy developing personae as good West Coast lefties to intervene in any important political critique.

As the film develops, London's and Oldham's performances, Reichardt's cinematography and editing, and Raymond's script indicate the danger of contemporary liberals' conflation of personal expression and political action. For example, the extended driving scene that dominates the film's initial fifteen minutes showcases the political implications of Reichardt's turn to neorealist film style. Known for its use of deep focus and on-location shooting, neorealism's setting and cinematography revealed the socioeconomic contexts in which its characters struggled for existence. In *Old Joy*, Reichardt uses a similar strategy in order to disclose a reality Kurt and Mark don't fully engage. As they exit Portland and then its outskirts, the camera initially shoots the two men from the side, keeping them in the frame as they converse. Passing through the city's Northwest Industrial Area, Kurt's gaze remains mostly on the marijuana in his lap, and Mark focuses on the road immediately ahead of him; but the camera's position allows the passing landscape to remain visible outside the windows as they talk. Reichardt's choice to shoot from within the vehicle—a technique that reappears throughout her œuvre—has the effect of immersing viewer in the environment. But in her films such shots additionally signify a view *refused*—one available to her characters, but not taken up by them.

Reichardt's insistence on treating the topography of her films with the same weight she treats her characters exposes the neoliberal landscape as one of a slow unfolding, whether the characters recognize this significance or not. Seeming to give up on the friends' ability to notice their environment, the camera shifts position midway through this long driving scene—it is important to note, when the men describe economic change in personal terms. Kurt brings up his money-making scheme of selling old music at a friend's record store, but Mark informs him, "Syd's [store] is gone, man. The rent got to be too heavy. Now it's a smoothie place. 'Rejuicenation.' Syd sells on eBay now." As Kurt murmurs "No more Syd's . . .," Reichardt cuts to a new camera position, pointing directly outside the window and eliminating the men from the frame. When Kurt finishes his thought by declaring "end of an era," Reichardt's

Figure 4: A view refused from *Old Joy* |

images make his point in a much more expansive way. In the sequence of tracking shots that then follows, no more dialogue can be heard and the friends do not appear—making clear that these are not subjective views. We watch as the landscape changes from urban industrial, to the shipping yards on the edge of town, to farm communities made up of trailer homes and rusty equipment, and then to logging trucks. All appear depopulated, with no workers visible, no machines moving. The sequence lasts two minutes, building a divide between viewers' and characters' perspectives. What Mark and Kurt understand as "the end of an era" is simply what has happened to them, to their friends, to their friendship; the dilapidated structures we see out the window index the end of an economic system. As Reichardt shows, a focus on the self and one's feelings of righteousness often prevents the emergency landscape that created the situation of personal crisis from coming into view.

All of Reichardt's neo-neorealist films undermine her characters' senses of themselves as agential and emphasize the way they are subject to structures they may not see, but *Old Joy* is unique for its exploration of the kind of self-absorption that makes such blindness possible. Kurt first appears in the film via a voicemail inviting his old friend on a hike to the hot springs. When he appears in bodily form, Kurt explains that he called Mark because he had a dream about him—setting the tone for the vague, New-Agey worldview that dominates his dialogue. Later, in the car, Kurt utters a typical placeholder statement: "You can't get real quiet anymore." He goes on to brag, "I visited this hot spring in Arizona last summer where no one is allowed to talk at all. Total silence. It was fucking amazing. They want me to come back and work as a chef sometime. I've got a whole menu worked out for 'em." Daniel London's delivery of the line, "Right, I think I read about that place in a magazine," reveals Mark's skepticism toward Kurt's "amazing" experience.

But collecting "amazing" experiences seems to be what Kurt's thirty-something existence consists of. Asking Mark whether he remembers a mutual friend named Yogi (he does; Yogi stiffed them on rent), Kurt relays yet another "amazing" adventure of life off the beaten path: "I ran into him in Big Sur last month. We had the most incredible night together. We were out under the stars. Dancing to these drums. Everyone was jumping over these huge bonfires. I'd never seen anything like it. Everyone was just so joyful that night. Beautiful women singing and dancing. I don't know, just a really, really amazing group of people."

Reichardt undercuts the patter of "amazings," "joyfuls," and "incredibles" with her framing and editing. She uses a variation of a shot-reverse-shot pattern to separate Mark and Kurt; unlike a typical shot-reverse-shot schema, however, the characters do not look toward another, but maintain a gaze straight ahead—a visual reflection of the way Kurt's chatter about his extreme lifestyle drives a wedge between the car's community of two. As Reichardt alternates between close-ups of the two men, she reveals Mark's tight jaw and slight eye roll as he listens to and becomes increasingly alienated by Kurt's bragging. Here, tales of Kurt's lifestyle choice do not bring joy to his audience, the responsible Mark, who, we can reasonably assume, covered Yogi's rent. Moreover, despite his claims to connect with resort owners in Arizona and beautiful women in Big Sur, Kurt is clearly alone. His possessions piled into a large van, Kurt has called up a friend with whom he has lost touch in the hope of producing another "amazing" adventure—fodder for more stories to substantiate his image. In many ways, Kurt is like a more culturally savvy Cozy; similar both in his attempt to escape the daily grind through romantic adventure and in his obliviousness to the costs his pursuits may have on those around him.

Different though they are, Kurt and Mark both show the self-absorption of contemporary leftists that leads them to focus on their individual choices, rather than the broader causes of the slow deterioration captured by Reichardt's neo-neorealism. Although Kurt annoyingly maintains the countercultural lifestyle of the duo's youth, Mark shows us what it looks like when the Seattle and Portland grunge and punk scenes grow up—and it's not much better, in Reichardt's view. A conversation late in the film shows the way that Mark's more adult leftist activism takes its place within the very neorealist structures that maintain the status quo he is ostensibly trying to remedy. Describing a volunteer teaching experience, Mark enthuses, "It's only one day a week, but it really pulls me out of myself. The kids are cool. They're really into it. And it's fun thinking about carpentry and woodworking in a way I haven't for a long time. It makes you realize how long ago sixteen was." Mark continues, "So now all this, what was a dumping ground, is now this really happening community garden." When Kurt enthuses, "I'm so proud of you, Mark. I'm serious. You've really done something, you've really given something back to the community," it seems overblown. And Mark's modesty in return—"Aww, I don't know"—rings false. But Kurt's praise goes on: "it's really something." By playing out a bit too long and a bit too grandly, these accolades become horrible when measured against the minor intervention of Mark's good works. The discomfort peaks when Mark passive-aggressively turns Kurt's compliments into a criticism of his friend, saying, "It's nothing you couldn't do if you felt like it, too. Not that you don't give back to the community. It's just a different community." After these remarks, the scene continues with twenty seconds of silence, during which Kurt walks ahead of Mark, motivating Reichardt's camera to follow him, visually isolating the friends from each other. Beyond the visual separation that occurs at this moment, Raymond's dialogue also reveals the displacement of care for the economically precarious that occurs in the millennial neoliberal moment, as activism becomes what one does if he "feels like it" and "community" looks like an increasingly fractured set of subcultures—which, as the end of the film makes clear, are incapable of offering real care for the down-and-out.

Here, again, Reichardt's shift from the psychological realism of *River of Grass* to an updated neorealism is crucial: Her later films reveal the broader social, political, economic, and environmental contexts in which her deeply flawed characters exist. In *Old Joy*, Reichardt's use of long shots and long takes—especially, tracking shots from inside moving vehicles that show passing landscapes—and on-location shooting allow her to undercut the friends' sense of their interventions in their local communities. Against the backdrop of the Pacific Northwest's devastated industrial landscape, Mark's volunteer gig painfully satirizes contemporary U.S. liberals: his commitments are those held by a comfortable middle class that prefers local and craft items and that positions community gardens as a solution to a failing local economy. In *Old Joy*, Reichardt offers no solution, just a painfully self-aware critique of Mark's sense of heroism in teaching woodworking to inner-city kids—a skill that can be only a boutique hobby, rather than a trade, in the film's postindustrial, largely postlogging Pacific Northwest landscape. Not unlike Cozy's romantic recasting of herself and Lee as a latter-day Bonnie and Clyde, Mark and Kurt paint themselves as heroes fighting the good lefty fight. But Reichardt's cinematography and Raymond's script puncture the delusion. *Old Joy*'s neo-neorealist attention to the Pacific Northwest's broader place in global economic and environmental processes reveal Mark's participation in gentrification and community improvement to be complicit in neoliberalism, as he embodies the shifting of government programs to more privatized modes of care.

Of course, the Oregon coast had been failing long before Mark and Kurt came of age. In one of Mark's more extended scenes of listening to Air America, Reichardt provides viewers with a short history of leftist politics in the second half of the twentieth century, one that helps to explain the contemporary left's inability to address the present-day economic emergencies she engages. The camera is trained out the window when Mark drives to pick up Kurt, capturing neighborhoods that decline in wealth from the cozy bungalows of Mark's block to housing projects and abandoned buildings. The soundscape that accompanies the scene refers to the defection of the white working class, traditionally the base of Old Left politics, from the Democratic Party. A caller to the radio program declares, "I never could understand why Lyndon Johnson became the champion of the civil-rights movement." He goes on to state that the Voting Rights Act "became the foundation of the Southern Strategy"—the Republican Party's successful attempts to court Southern Democrats by appealing to their racism toward African Americans. One of the commentators agrees, noting that Johnson said, "'we've delivered the South to the Republican Party for a long time' when he signed the act." "But he said it with regret," the other commentator chimes in. "These were all wedge issues," the first commentator concludes. Thereby, the film reminds us of how working-class whites were pitted against poor people of color in a way that obfuscated their similarities in terms of class. Arguably, the New Left's failure to attend to the financial concerns of working-class or downwardly mobile whites allowed the Right to successfully exploit racial tensions and capture these voters. These points might help explain why Reichardt's cinematic worlds, as concerned as they are with vulnerability and suffering, can be so overwhelmingly white—and why every one of her films since *River of Grass* explicitly depicts a fringe character who refuses to sympathize with another fringe character. Like all Reichardt's protagonists to date, Mark and Kurt are white, a fact of demography in her films important for understanding her cinema as particular to contemporary economic and political contexts. In her work on cruel optimism as an affective mode specific to the current moment, Berlant has explained, "People born into unwelcoming worlds and unreliable environments have a different response to the new precarities than do people who presumed they would be protected" (20). It is on these unsuspecting members of the new precariat that Reichardt focuses, those who thought they were the inheritors of the very narratives of U.S. self-efficacy that Reichardt has devoted her career to dismantling.

The end of *Old Joy* crystallizes these failures of identification while also suggesting the ultimate failure of Mark and Kurt's reunion; they will not, we suspect, ever see each other again. This end also previews Reichardt's work in her next film, *Wendy and Lucy*, which retains neorealism's loose causality but moves away from its traditional use of deep focus. In *Old Joy*'s last ten minutes, the friends drive back to Portland as night falls. When they approach town, only the car's headlights and the lights of the city illuminate the scene, including a neon billboard picked out by Reichardt's camera, boasting, "Made in Oregon." This slogan can be read only as ironic in light of the landscapes seen in the daylight drive out of town: a region abandoned by industry. Pulling over to a curb, Mark lets Kurt out of the car and the men exchange a series of pleasant lies. "That was, that was awesome, Kurt," Mark enthuses. "I'll call you soon, man," Kurt replies. As soon as Mark pulls away, he switches the radio back on. A voice opines, "It's not going to take care of the new people that come along every year to join the labor force or to rejoin it." The film ends, however, not with Mark's driving home, but with our discovery that the house where we thought Kurt was being deposited is not a home at all—a discovery that, it seems, Mark chooses not to face. When Mark drops Kurt off, Kurt opens and passes through a door that leads to a backyard or alleyway. But when the film returns to him for its final minutes, we see him aimlessly wandering the streets of one of Portland's seedier districts, offering a visual correspondence to the radio voice's worry about people for whom there appears to be no room in a productive U.S. society with few remaining safety nets. As Kurt walks, the camera tracks and pans, keeping him in view, but from a distance, positioned across the street. Employing shallow focus, the camera makes the environment press upon Kurt. In this final scene, the camera takes on something akin to Mark's disinterested view of his friend—or, more broadly, what might be construed as a kind of neoliberal view of those who can't make it in the U.S. workforce; cars pass in front of Kurt and he goes in and out of focus. Finally, the camera comes to a stop, as though tired of tracking Kurt. He walks out of the frame altogether and the words "Old Joy," now ironic, come up onscreen.

Figure 5: Kurt and a homeless man share a look in *Old Joy*

Although *Old Joy*'s final moments depart from typical neorealist visual style, its closing retains neorealist narration's emphasis on the accidental nature of catastrophes for someone like Kurt. In his last onscreen appearance, Kurt interacts with a homeless man who is dressed very similarly. As the two men momentarily stand side by side, both bearded, both wearing nondescript tan jackets, their visual correspondence discloses the short distance between their situations. Reichardt's habit of depicting the relatively arbitrary difference between doing okay and total desperation is yet another inheritance from her neorealist forbears. Writing of *Bicycle Thieves*, Bazin asserts, "Nothing happens in *Ladri di Biciclette* that *might just as well not have happened*. . . . The marvelous aesthetic paradox of this film is that it has the relentless quality of tragedy while *nothing happens in it except by chance*" ("De Sica," 68, our emphasis). That is, things feel tragic, but without the catalysts of tragedy: a curse, say, or a fatal flaw. Instead, in De Sica's film, everything hinges on the titular bicycle. Similarly minimal objects in Reichardt's films—a serpentine belt (*Wendy and Lucy*) or a barrel of water (*Meek's Cutoff*)—mean the difference between precarious life and out-and-out disaster. In her take on Bazin, Jennifer Fay parses this paradox of neorealism's contingent plots by explaining that "neorealist films feature individuals whose accidental lives are beholden to seemingly immutable social forces" (48). It is because of this paradox that we would slightly revise Bazin to call Reichardt's cinema that of emergency, not tragedy; it has *the relentless quality of emergency*, in the sense of ever-unfolding and ever-threatening troubles. Though not describing the film movement, Berlant's account of the way crises unfold today—as "the emergence of something in the present that *may* become an event" (5, emphasis ours)—maps nicely onto the stakes of Reichardt's neo-neorealist plotting. Much as De Sica did in the 1940s and 1950s, Reichardt's films in the 2000s show how easy it is for one accident to knock a person out of society; incidents in her films *may* become life-threatening events, but, just as easily, they may not. Indeed, *Old Joy*'s Mark might have followed his old friend's Kurt's path, and Kurt lives one mishap away from the life of the homeless man.

The distinction between tragedy and emergency, and its implications for thinking through economic crises, is most apparent in Reichardt's *Wendy and Lucy*, an update of De Sica's neorealist classic *Umberto D.*

This 2008 film picks up where *Old Joy*, which hints that its protagonist Kurt may be currently or imminently homeless, leaves off. Focused on a young woman named Wendy and her dog Lucy, it begins with its title characters already homeless, living in a car as they make their way out to the Alaskan fish canneries. When they hit Oregon, the car breaks down and Wendy shoplifts, gets arrested, and loses Lucy, each new crisis further depleting her already thin roll of dollars and increasing her desperation. Reichardt shows U.S. bureaucracy to be complicit in this process, chipping away at Wendy's money as well as her time: We watch as Wendy files forms, pays fees, and waits around in both the jail and the pound, institutional spaces for housing down-and-out living creatures. Tracking the process by which a young woman free-falls out of the working class, in a world with no safety nets to catch her, Reichardt again eschews a focus on a psychological realism in favor of a more neorealist style of plotting. In his article on *Meek's Cutoff*, James Lattimer has described her use of neorealist plotting as one that causes audiences to reflect on the thin line between incidents that are causal and those that are merely chronological, noting that her narratives are "structured as a series of episodes whose relationship to one another moves constantly back and forth between the 'then' and the 'therefore'" (38). It is important to note that what counts as a "then" or a "therefore" varies according to one's social position. Reichardt's neo-neorealism thereby suggests the cruelty of our contemporary everyday emergency state: Wendy has no revealed fatal flaw that justifies her punishments; she's merely a woman in a precarious circumstance who experiences one problem too many. Indeed, the film could easily be described, in Bazin's terms, as a series of accidents that need not have happened.

Finally, while classical tragedy emphasizes immutable character flaws that lead to bad decision making, the concept of emergency emphasizes mutable environmental contexts (hurricanes, recessions) that delimit human choice. Reichardt's resistance to affective appeals may be one way of understanding the lack of backstory for Wendy, as well as for her other post–*River of Grass* protagonists. We receive only a few clues about her past, which largely come in the form of her marked-up map and financial ledger. These documents index her growing precarity, and through their factual, rather than emotional, detail leave us to focus on her *conditions*, not her *personality*. Though we cannot perceive much personalizing information through Wendy's unspectacular opacity, we can begin to see how the relatively simplistic plotlines, unflashy style, environmental focus, and process-oriented plots of Kelly Reichardt's neo-neorealism make ethical appeals without tugging the heartstrings.

Precarity: *Wendy and Lucy*

Todd Haynes, the renowned U.S. indie writer-director and frequent Kelly Reichardt producer, has noted that the latter's films are "all sort of failed road movies" (Hornaday). Reichardt's first four features bear recognizable markers of that genre—whether the plot device of the journey that promises both a change of circumstances and a change of scenery or scenes of characters consulting maps and encountering random strangers. But the films' failures to conform to the road genre's tropes are as prominent as their adherence to them.[23] In *River of Grass*, our protagonists attempt to change their dull, stifling lives by engaging in a crime spree that proves quite short-range, their flight out of Miami ultimately thwarted. In *Old Joy*, old friends Mark and Kurt attempt but fail to reconnect on a weekend hiking trip—which, like the trajectory of *River of Grass*, is literally and figuratively circular. In *Wendy and Lucy*, our protagonist's main goal is to drive to Alaska from Indiana and land a paying gig that will turn her life around, but her car is dead on our arrival. In *Meek's Cutoff*, a wagon train of would-be pioneers from back East finds themselves lost in the maddeningly unvarying Oregon desert.

The road movie, as we are hinting, concerns much more than just geographical movement: it is a genre about aspiration and optimism. As Wendy Everett reminds us, "In America, road movies [have] tapped into a potent cultural myth in which notions of the open road and travel reflect a fundamental belief in 'the freedom to move upward and outward'" (166, quoting Eyerman and Löfgren). More than simply exploding these myths and beliefs, Reichardt attends to their perverse endurance: While clinging to the belief that they can escape their circumstances, many of Reichardt's characters end up merely spinning their wheels, sometimes quite literally. In *Meek's Cutoff*, for example, Emily Tetherow asks her husband Solomon, "What if we don't find water soon?" "We will," he replies. "Your optimism," she mutters, exasperated. But later, Emily has come to put faith in the Native American man that the group has essentially kidnapped, and more specifically in his ability to lead the group to water. Solomon asks Emily, "Do you think he's trustworthy?" "The Indian? You're doubtful," she observes. "I have my doubts," he confirms. The stark reversal of their positions is made clear when, as the man begins speaking and gesturing near the film's end, Emily veritably enthuses, "He says we're close. He says we're almost there"—thus echoing a scene in *Old Joy*, when the two friends have lost their way and a naive Kurt insists to an exasperated Mark, "We're super close" (a misguided comment that could also be read metaphorically, in terms of the pair's friendship). The fact that no single individual in *Meek's Cutoff* can maintain a sense of hope long-term suggests optimism's simultaneous flimsiness and durability: its ineffectualness and its crushing psychic weight; the way that it becomes untenable and yet will not die. Throughout her œuvre, Reichardt indicts optimism as a dangerous ideology.

Meek's Cutoff addresses U.S. optimism in an older era of precarity; *Wendy and Lucy*, in contrast, is Reichardt's most timely and incisive account of this process: It appeared in December 2008, three months after the massive financial meltdown that continues to reverberate across the globe. We note, first, how Reichardt employs dramatic irony to both indict cruel optimism—what Lauren Berlant defines as "a relation of attachment to compromised conditions of possibility" (24)—and demonstrate how it flourishes under precarity. We then discuss how Reichardt's films concern themselves with the fate of personal relationships under precarity—why interconnectivity and interdependence come to look like risks, threats, or burdens under such conditions, and how commitments to people, places, and animals come to be unsustainable. Again, Reichardt asks what obligations we have to others in a time of economic downturn, scarcity, and neoliberalism; a time at which the *private*, not the *communal*, is still stressed as the best path to success.

Wendy and Lucy tracks the ever-growing troubles of Wendy Carroll, a young woman from Indiana who has stopped in Oregon en route to Alaska, where she hopes to find work in a cannery. After a night sleeping in her car in a Walgreens parking lot, Wendy is awakened by a security guard (Walter Dalton), who asks her to move. When she discovers that her car is dead, the dominoes begin to fall: concerned that her tightly plotted budget will not hold up, Wendy shoplifts food for her dog Lucy and is caught and sent to jail. While she remains in custody, Lucy runs away. The rest of the film consists of Wendy's mundane actions: waiting to be released from jail, waiting to hear about the cost of her car repairs, waiting to hear from the pound about Lucy's whereabouts, and interacting with various locals and strangers. She eventually finds Lucy, but her car repairs turn out to exceed her means and she decides to leave the dog with a foster family. The film's last shot gives us a glimpse of Wendy's grim face as she rides the rails to who knows where.

Perhaps it is surprising that Reichardt has described the film as being inspired by Hurricane Katrina. As she told fellow filmmaker Gus Van Sant:

> The seeds of *Wendy and Lucy* happened shortly after Hurricane Katrina, after hearing talk about people pulling themselves up by their bootstraps, and hearing the presumption that people's lives were so precarious due to some laziness on their part. Jon and I were musing on the idea of having no net—let's say your bootstraps floated away—how do you get out of your situation totally on your own without help from the government? We were watching a lot of Italian neo-realism and thinking the themes of those films seem to ring true for life in America in the Bush years. There's a certain kind of help that society will give and a certain help it won't give.

The specter of Katrina vis-à-vis the film invokes an obvious problem: Wendy is white, but we know that the dispossessed of Katrina were overwhelmingly black. We find two ways to think through this problematic comparison. First, we have established how Reichardt's film *Old Joy* critiques leftist failures and have noted specifically how the Air America scenes in that film point to the misguidedness of the white working class's defection from the political left. To put a fine point on it: In offering a protagonist who is precarious despite her whiteness, *Wendy and Lucy* reminds us of how the political right in the United States has managed to co-opt people like Wendy: those who aspire to become wealthy or, at least, to lift themselves up by their bootstraps on their own, despite ample evidence that doing so is largely impossible. Second, most accounts of the precariat—the new socioeconomic class in which we locate Wendy—specifically cite the relatively new, and "surprising," precarity of white, middle-class citizens. Indeed, we might identify 2008's *Wendy and Lucy* with works such as Jess Walter's novel *The Financial Lives of the*

Poets, which appeared a year later, as a text that captures what Barbara Ehrenreich has called the middle class's "fear of falling."[24] Here, we do not mean to suggest that race is irrelevant when it comes to situations of precarity. But Reichardt helps us see how, in contemporary states of emergency, the protections of race—and the class into which one was born, and aspiration, and hard work—may not be the reliable protections one might hope.

It is important to note that Wendy does not recognize this. Although there is much that we as viewers don't know in any Reichardt film,[25] our filmmaker ensures that there is much that we do know, and that her characters do not—thus creating dramatic irony. In this way, Reichardt ensures that we do not share in her characters' hopes. These characters articulate discourses of progress, of certainty, though we see that their lives are in fact defined by diminishment, unpredictability. They insist that they are exceptional, when we know that they are just one of many on the economic brink. For example, when we watch Wendy proclaim to various people she encounters that she's going to make it to Alaska, find work at a cannery, and start making good money, we as audience members know better because of Reichardt's choices.[26] For one thing, the film has started in medias res, with Wendy's car already dead. Mobility has *never* been a feature of Wendy's onscreen existence, thus preventing us from wishing for that feature to be restored, as classic narrative form would have it. Moreover, we lack a visually established point of origin for this character, a site against which we might pit her intended endpoint of Alaska. We do know, from a quick shot of her budget and a brief reference to her license plates, that she's from Indiana, but we never see her there. Reichardt thus does not encourage us to wish that Wendy could escape that home—or, alternately, that she could return to it. Reichardt also occasionally engages in visual irony as a means of creating dramatic irony, thus further throwing our protagonist's plans in doubt. For example, one scene features Wendy, on her way to put up lost-dog fliers for Lucy, striding purposefully past a wall covered with the large graffito that reads "Goner." Looking straight ahead, Wendy literally does not read the writing on the wall.

We might also recognize dramatic irony in our protagonist's mantra, uttered in several variations throughout the film: "I'm not from here—I'm just passing through." In one sense, this statement is tragically ironic, insofar as we've seen Wendy fail over and over, day by day, to "pass through" this small town and reach her goal of Alaska. Her desperate act of shoplifting dog food, meant to sustain her companion on the rest of their journey, only extends her familiarity with the town: It lands her in the local jail for several hours and then takes her back to the store again, where she was forced to leave her dog when she was arrested. And the system threatens to pull her back into this town's orbit in the future; when she is released from jail, the clerk tells her, "You can pay your fine now, or you come back in two weeks for a trial with a judge. Then you can pay the $50, plus court fees." When Wendy protests that she doesn't live there, the woman warns, "If you get stopped in another state, you're just going to end up right back here."[27] But Wendy's mantra is ironic in another sense: as far as the plotline goes, and as far as our viewing relationship with Wendy goes, she actually is, if not "*from* here," simply *here*. That is, we see her operate in one context only, that of the small Oregon town where all the film's action takes place, with no flashbacks, no establishing shots from an earlier time or place, no "six months later" epilogues. She is a classic stranger with a twist: ubiquitous and, thus, not particularly mysterious, as she establishes routines and patterns in relation to local landmarks and denizens. (We might therefore contrast her with well-known stranger characters from U.S. film, from the righteous veteran John Macreedy [Spencer Tracy], who receives a hostile reception from a corrupt town in *Bad Day at Black Rock* [dir. John Sturges, 1955], to the sexy maybe-murderer Josh [Robert John Burke] who rolls into town in *The Unbelievable Truth* [dir. Hal Hartley, 1989.]) Indeed, even the film's final shot, which finds Wendy grimly climbing into a moving boxcar—and which might otherwise indicate her ultimate mobility or even success—does not last long enough for her to have moved beyond the confines of the town by the film's conclusion. Until the very end, Wendy is "here."

To be clear, small-town Oregon does not seem like a viable home for Wendy. For one thing, the bleakness of her surroundings suggests a lack of local employment opportunities. In a rare moment of conversation with the security guard, this suggestion is confirmed: Wendy remarks, "not a lot of jobs around here, huh?" and the guard responds, "I'll say. I don't know what the people do all day. Used to be a mill, but it's been closed a long time now"—a hint to the Pacific Northwest's postindustrial economic and environmental decline that, as we have suggested, greatly interests Reichardt. In her take on the film, Gorfinkel has noted the way Wendy is often framed against decaying economic environments that visualize "the dead time of postindustrial arrest . . . the hypostasis of manufacturing" ("Weariness," 335). The environment's stagnancy is mirrored, if unknowingly, by Wendy herself, as well as by the newly precarious white working class with which she identifies. Our point, then, is not that Wendy should embrace the small town in which she finds herself trapped. We wish merely to point out that, although Wendy doesn't "live [t]here," she also doesn't live anywhere else. The cruel bind of the film is that our protagonist cannot leave the place that has nothing to offer her—thus upending ideologies of bootstrap advancement and U.S. dreaming: the idea that good, industrious people can make it if they just try.

More than simply not recognizing her downward mobility, Wendy seems gripped by cruel optimism. In one scene, she arrives at a recycling center with a few cans to find a long line of itinerant individuals chatting patiently (the length of the line serving as another sign, we might say, of the bleakness of the town in which she finds herself). She brushes off one man's offer to recycle her cans for her and give her the money later. She tells him, "you can just take them; it's fine" and then leaves abruptly. In such moments, she makes a bold, largely unfounded, and thus cruelly optimistic declaration: *Actually, I'm doing okay; you might need the money—or the camaraderie—but I don't.* Her gestures serve as protective and ideological disidentifications, emerging from her pressing need to believe that she is harder-working, wiser, and, therefore, better off than those on the skids. She needs to believe not only that there is a fundamental difference between them, but that she is doing something different and, thus, will get a different outcome.

And, of course, with her dream of going to the canneries to gain a financial foothold, Wendy is nothing if not an upwardly aspiring character. Her daily routines express those aspirations, establishing a distinction between the home that her car has become and her "workday," which includes taking care of various bits of business: cleaning herself up at a gas station sink, changing a bandage on her ankle (another sign of precarity), checking in at the dog shelter, visiting the coffee shop, stopping by the Walgreens. These routines ape those associated with middle-class respectability: go to work, come home, start again. We can then understand Wendy's attempts to make her time productive as efforts to rise above the multivalent category of "wastrel": both a person who wastes time, and a person whom society treats as waste. Put another way, her optimism, which grows cruel over the course of the film, is specifically articulated through her attempts to manage time. (See the discussion of Schoonover in our "Duration" section that follows.) Thus, while Wendy's routines share a pointlessness with those of characters such as *River of Grass*'s Cozy and *Old Joy*'s Kurt—once she puts up signs for her missing dog, for example, she could just wait in the car—her habit of devising things to do is aspirational. Wendy's inevitable decline is, therefore, all the more devastating and all the more painful to watch: As a young woman in the mid-oughts, she resonates with that new class of the downwardly mobile, raised on the dreams and habits of the U.S. middle class, but with none of the structures in place through which to achieve such dreams. Perhaps, then, we might read one of Stephen Meek's declarations in *Meek's Cutoff* as having contemporary political resonance, despite its appearance as a geographical reference in that 1845-set text: "This country'll play tricks on you. That piece you see out there might be a whole lot farther than you think."

Reichardt further explores Wendy's precarity through depictions of interconnectivity and interdependence—and, more specifically, a lack

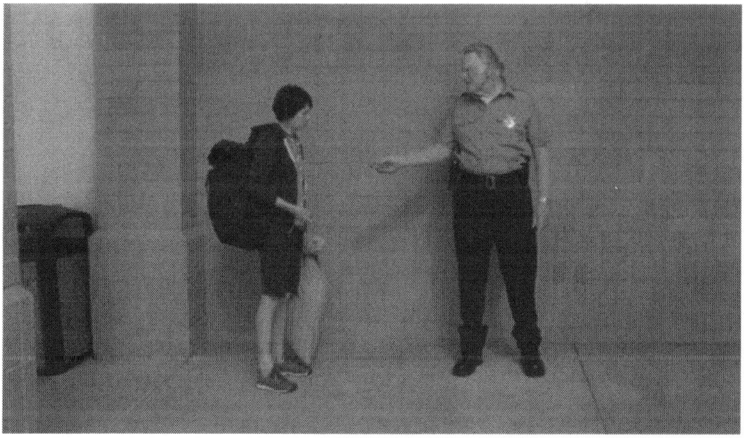

Figure 6: Offering Wendy a phone in *Wendy and Lucy*

thereof. Wendy routinely fails to build connections with others, a failure that at first seems to be an issue of individual disposition; while her economic situation, compounded by her solitude, is bleak indeed, she bristles at the possibilities of community that are tendered to her. For example, when the kindly Walgreens security guard offers her both the use of his cell phone and some extra money, she initially tries to resist and then only begrudgingly accepts—realizing, it seems, that doing so means that she is connected to him through the feelings of obligation or gratitude. *Meek's Cutoff* depicts a similar dynamic: When Emily Tetherow (also, like Wendy, played by Michelle Williams) fixes the Native American man's moccasin, she tells one of her fellow would-be settlers, Millie, "I want him to owe me something." As Emily suggests, and as Wendy seems to know, the opposite situation—owing something to someone else—makes you vulnerable. The group members in *Meek's* cooperate among themselves, sharing bread and making room in their wagons, but they do not want to be beholden or obligated to a stranger. If one *must* have a relationship with this figure, Reichardt's characters seem to believe, it should be purely instrumental.

Reichardt shows these refusals of connectivity and community to be ultimately rooted in larger structural factors rather than individual personality. She thereby challenges the cinematic small-town fantasies that structure so many pre–Great Recession road movies, from *Doc Hollywood* (dir. Michael Caton-Jones, 1991) to *Priscilla, Queen of the Desert* (dir. Stephan Elliott, 1994)—in which strangers are easily and happily folded into the communities they accidentally encounter, finding work, friends, love, and other sustaining resources. (We should also think here of how *Certain Women*'s loosely interconnected small-town characters brush past each other; strangers to one another even despite their common geography.) To begin with the obvious, Wendy cuts a vulnerable figure. Slight, female, and, except for her sometime-companion Lucy, all alone, her wariness of strangers is quite understandable. Moreover, as the security guard makes plain, there is no work to be found in town, no immediate opportunity, much less reason, for Wendy to stick around and improvise a life. In the reality of scarcity faced by figures such as Wendy and the *Meek's* travelers, one cannot—or, at least, one *feels* that one cannot—afford to trust others, sometimes quite literally. Screenwriter Jon Raymond's short story version of *Wendy and Lucy*, "Train

Choir," makes this point quite explicit: When the security guard offers his cell phone, the protagonist wonders "if she would have to pay for this gesture someday" (240). *Wendy and Lucy* captures this sentiment mostly through framing and actors' body language; standing the same distance from the edges of the frame, facing each other, Wendy steps backward from the security guard when he offers his cell phone. When she finally accepts the telephone, Reichardt cuts in to a tighter shot of Wendy's face, rueful and abashed.

We might even read Wendy's standoffishness with the security guard extradiegetically—as symbolizing a resentment, perhaps not consciously felt by the character herself, of the economic competition that this older figure represents. The dynamic between this underemployed older security guard and the unemployed young woman, in fact, indexes a widespread global trend of the early twenty-first century. The elimination of traditional pension plans, along with investment losses triggered by the recent crash, have created a scenario in which older people have little hope of retiring. This aging workforce that shows no sign of leaving the labor market, in turn, forecloses opportunities for younger generations. Perhaps more to the diegetic point, the first thing Wendy does when she reaches relative safety after a terrifying encounter with a mentally ill man in the woods is unhook and remove the money belt hidden under her clothes; while the encounter seems to threaten our protagonist with physical or even sexual assault, Reichardt keeps Wendy's financial concerns utterly vivid. She thereby asks us to consider such characters' seeming misanthropy or snobbery as something more, or something else: as survival or self-protection mechanisms. Moreover, she invites us to consider how conditions of emergency and scarcity do not necessarily unite the downtrodden but can in fact viciously divide them.

Although Wendy's presence, as a stranger-outsider, tests others' hospitality, generosity, openness, and sense of obligation, her own generosity, openness, and sense of obligation, if not hospitality, are tested by others. People make demands on her, not just the other way around—from the crust punks, men at the recycling center, and security guard all trying to engage her in conversation and companionship, to the stock boy, manager, and mechanic who all insist, with varying degrees of rigidity, that she has engaged in a transaction with them, and, therefore, owes them something. Thus, although *Wendy and Lucy* explores how townspeople will treat a stranger, it also explores how a stranger will treat townspeople. It seems that both parties, the individual stranger-outsider and the community's local-insider, have the potential to reject the other, though the former is always more vulnerable, stripped as she is of support and resources. And, in fact, while Wendy is largely accepted by those she encounters—engaged by the crust punks and men at the recycling center, given money and a telephone by the security guard, granted a discount by the mechanic[28]—she largely rejects them. Such rejections, as we have been suggesting, are shaped by both material circumstances and ideological ones; by what one has or doesn't have, as well as what one believes one should, could, or will have. In a time of precarity, Reichardt shows us, community often shrinks.

More specifically, *Wendy and Lucy* alludes to how, in a post–Citizens United world, the corporation has come to stand in for the community—specifically, how corporations have transformed public perceptions such that they can now be understood as person, as benefactor, as benevolent paternal force. Consider, for example, how Wendy parks her car in the Walgreens parking lot to sleep, thereby invoking the phenomenon of Walmart camping, a product of the corporation's policy of allowing recreational vehicles and other vehicles to park overnight. (Raymond, in "Train Choir," actually refers to the Walgreens parking lot as the "best *camping* option Verna [the Wendy analogue in the story] had been able to find" [211].) The Walmart policy has become such an institution that roadtrippers can now purchase a Walmart-brand road atlas that comes with a pocket publication titled *Wherezitat? Locate-a-Walmart*. These publications are a fine index of how the corporation, and late capitalism more broadly, steps in to offer hospitality where it otherwise does not exist: "Wherever I go, I can always find a Walmart." The extent to which such texts have garnered corporations like Walmart the reputation of caring for the public, including the itinerant, is apparent in the user comments on websites like Freecampgrounds.com—as is the extent to which the public *wants to believe* that corporations care. One camper, "Dan," testifies,

> We have stayed in a number of Walmarts and have been welcomed with open arms. Management even alerts security to keep [an] eye on the rigs during a stay. If you have a wife like mine (Walmart road atlas in hand) she

> always needs something from the store. If we stay in a Super Walmart we always hit the deli for a good chicken dinner with potato salad and cole slaw.

These commenters clearly construe the store's policies as generous hospitality rather than bald commercialism.[29]

Of course, Wendy's corporate camping doesn't last long; the morning after what appears to be her first night, the Walgreens security guard asks her to leave, despite the complete emptiness of the lot. But the fact remains that Reichardt places her in the Walgreens lot in the first place—as opposed to, say, the family grocery store where she later shops. Even though the acts of hospitality that do take place in Reichardt's films actually come from members of the local community sharing meager resources—Kurt's monetary gift to the homeless man in *Old Joy* and the security guard's offer to Wendy of a telephone and money—Reichardt depicts characters who tend to put their faith in the larger system instead. Doing so, the films suggest, is a response to the abject sense of powerlessness and random fate that the larger system creates.

When plans and expectations eventually fail, Reichardt shows us, those on the economic brink lose not only their material possessions and resources but also their preexisting emotional and interpersonal ties—perhaps another reason that characters such as Wendy are loath to build new ties in the first place. Here, again, we see Reichardt's ironic inflection of the road movie. That genre is so often focused on the (supposed) freedom from material and interpersonal ties—such as Jack Nicholson leaving his pregnant girlfriend in a gas station diner in *Five Easy Pieces* (dir. Bob Rafelson, 1970), *Thelma and Louise* ditching repressive routines and bad relationships, or Christopher McCandless disposing of all his earthly possessions before going *Into the Wild* (dir. Sean Penn, 2007)—but Reichardt, instead, shows the crushing devastation of these losses. Such paring down, in her œuvre, is not a lifestyle choice, not an exercise in self-restraint, not a freeing up of oneself from consumerism—as seen especially in the spate of yuppie road movies of the 1980s, such as *Lost in America* (dir. Albert Brooks, 1985), *Something Wild* (dir. Jonathan Demme, 1986), and *Rain Man* (dir. Barry Levinson, 1988)—nor a metaphor for the social mores one is leaving behind. Rather, it is an instance of the bare-knuckle frugality and survivalism under which so many live every day.

Nonhuman animals are key to Reichardt's meditation on the fate of relationships under precarity. (In our final section, we take up animals in a different sense, discussing the idea of animal survivors.) That is, she focuses not just on human ties and responsibilities, but those that cross species boundaries. Specifically, she considers the conditions under which those ties and responsibilities can be maintained, asking whether and how they can span changes in status, including declining fortunes. Wendy's precarious situation, of course, prompts her to cut her tie to her dog, Lucy. After traveling to the foster home where Lucy has been placed while Wendy was in jail, she plays fetch with the dog for a few moments before leaving in tears. We realize that our protagonist seems to have internalized the smug declaration of the stock boy who turns her in for shoplifting: "If you can't afford dog food then you shouldn't have a dog." *Meek's Cutoff* takes up these same questions, though more subtly. The second shot opens with two women crossing a river waist-deep; the second woman carries a basket on her head and the first carries a wooden birdcage housing a small bird. A later scene, filmed in close-up, shows the bird's owner, Millie, carefully pouring water from a tin into the bird's bowl. The animal's yellow color resonates against the woman's yellow dress and may remind viewers of Wendy's "yellow-gold" Labrador retriever. But by about an hour into *Meek's Cutoff* we see a shot of the empty birdcage swinging on the back of a wagon. No action or discussion indicates the once-cherished bird's fate to us, but the cage remains as a somber reminder of the emotional ties the group has been forced to cut. And it also indicates the grueling utilitarianism under which they exist: we can guess that the birdcage has been saved only for future use as firewood, a possibility suggested by the many previous scenes of brushwood gathering.

It's notable, we might argue, that Reichardt's real-life dog Lucy appears in both *Old Joy* and *Wendy and Lucy*: In the filmmaker's œuvre, Lucy indexes how economic circumstances shape possibilities for affective connections. In *Old Joy*, Lucy is Mark's dog—arguably another marker of middle-class comfort, along with his car, home, and pregnant wife. Indeed, when Kurt observes at one point that "your dog's in distress," Mark replies that his wife "calls it separation anxiety"; the domestic dog has even been psychologized. Thus, whereas in *Old Joy* she is mobile and comfortably middle-class, accompanying the men on their trip and then returning home to Mark's house, in the other film it seems that Wendy has been holding Lucy back from such a middle-class life. This difference between the two fictional Lucys makes the critical point that neoliberal society accepts affective relationships only to the extent that the participants can support them. The real tragedy of Wendy, then, is not her misanthropy but her place in a milieu of scarcity and privatization—a milieu in which both offers of, and requests for, help can be read as threats, and in which the development of community and connection is discouraged or feared at every turn.

Many critics have read *Wendy and Lucy* as an update of De Sica's *Umberto D.*, the classic neorealist tale of a pensioner and his dog. Both films feature characters obsessively tallying accounts, measuring in cash their distance from, or, perhaps, position within, crisis. Further, like Wendy with her romanticized Alaskan cannery job, Umberto D. counts on a magical inflow of money, in the form of a pension payment that will supposedly solve all his woes. Also like Wendy, Umberto D. is not entirely a blameless innocent; he has debts and he bends the rules to care for himself and for his little dog Flike—who, like Lucy, also winds up in a pound. It is important to note, though, as we have observed, Wendy is not a cuddly, cute old man like Umberto D. but rather sullen, prickly, and antisocial. (In fact, the only cuddly, cute old man in *Wendy and Lucy* is the Walgreens security guard Walter, whom Wendy treats largely with wary suspicion; Reichardt's relentless antisentimentality pushes the cuddly, cute old man figure into a literally thankless supporting role.) With a protagonist who thwarts easy emotional attachments, Reichardt extends neorealism's representation of those society sees as "too old or poor so they're a blight[;] they're like stray dogs" (Van Sant)—extends it, we might say, to the unlikable. Rather than encouraging identification with Wendy, then, Reichardt asks the viewer to consider the dignity and social responsibility owed to less-than-appealing figures and suggests that being sympathetic should not be a prerequisite for economic dignity. These films—*Umberto D.* as a post–World War II film and *Wendy and Lucy* as a post-Katrina film—implicate the government and the public in a failure of care.

The difference between the respective endings of the neo-neorealist *Wendy and Lucy* and its neorealist forebear *Umberto D.* are rather instructive in this way. When *Umberto D.* closes, the pensioner has rescued Flike from the pound before he was to be destroyed. The dog refuses to abandon his suicidal master, and the film ends with a heartwarming if uncertain reunification of the two. In comparison, *Wendy and Lucy* ends with far more certainty about its canine protagonist than its human one. Lucy has found a safe place by the end of the film, the foster home with plenty of food. In contrast, we find Wendy resorting to train-hopping, facing the future without money, car, or companionship. With this ending, Reichardt's revision of De Sica's neorealism draws uncomfortable attention to the reasons Flike and Lucy garner our sympathies: They evoke pathos in less complicated ways than their human owners, and their needs may be met without fundamentally changing social structures. Thus, in the literal economies, and the economies of emotion, that *Wendy and Lucy* critiques, Lucy the dog can be rescued from life on the street, but Wendy the human cannot.

And indeed, the local community in *Wendy and Lucy* seems ultimately more hospitable to a dog than to a girl.[30] The pound that houses Lucy is a place of cozy blankets and chew toys, a way station before a better life in adoption—in contrast to the grim cells of *Umberto D.* that threaten death. Meanwhile, the safest, most comfortable and clean place Wendy rests in the entire film is jail. "A night in the pound never hurt anyone," the security guard insists to a worried Wendy, which seems to

Figure 7: Wendy and Lucy "behind bars" in *Wendy and Lucy*

be true for both Wendy and Lucy. But a night—or a lifetime—trying to make it on one's own on the outside is another matter entirely. Here, we might see the ironic twists of the film's title: most would assume upon first encounter that "Wendy and Lucy" refers to two entities on equal ontological footing—specifically, two female humans, à la *Thelma and Louise*. As one begins to watch, however, one might think it refers to two entities on *un*equal ontological footing: an elevated human and her lower-status dog. But we conclude that we are watching two entities on unequal socioeconomic footing: a down-and-out human and her soon-to-be-middle-class dog. Reichardt seems to establish this point visually, shooting Wendy from Lucy's position within the foster-home yard, such that the human is framed through the chain-link fence. While it's Lucy who is literally behind bars, Reichardt shows Wendy as the one who is trapped. As the film closes, we know where Lucy will live. But we know as little about where Wendy is going as we do about where she has been.

Duration: *Meek's Cutoff*

Set in nineteenth-century Oregon Territory, *Meek's Cutoff* focuses on a small wagon train of three couples—Emily (Michelle Williams) and Solomon Tetherow (Will Patton), Millie (Zoe Kazan) and Thomas Gateley (Paul Dano), and Glory (Shirley Henderson) and William White (Neal Huff)—and their guide, Stephen Meek (Bruce Greenwood). With a screenplay drawn from the journals of real-life settlers, the film begins with its characters lost in the desert, running out of water, and increasingly distrustful of the man meant to lead them to western bounty. Tensions rise on the Oregon Trail when they encounter a man referred to as "the Indian"; will he bring the wagon train to water or to destruction? As its protagonists falter and fail, *Meek's* engages the western as a narrative genre that, much like the road movie, focuses on questions of mobility, openness, mastery, and American dreams. Reichardt's only period film to date, *Meek's* clarifies Reichardt's status as a chronicler of U.S. failure. Even when telling perhaps the most triumphant story Americans can tell (the settling of the West and, thus, the development of the United States in its current form), she focuses on the losers, those settlers who did not achieve the good life but likely perished on the way.

Meek's has earned a reputation not just as a revisionist western but, specifically, a "feminist Western"[31] for its interrogation of gender and power. *Meek's* is effectively absent the western's traditional white male hero; the titular figure here is the villain, and the other white men are at best circumspect and at worst weak and ineffectual. The film thereby collapses the western's typological distinctions, leaving Emily Tetherow and Rod Rondeaux's unnamed Native American character to emerge as the protagonists.[32] Despite eroding the role of the masculine hero, *Meek's* shows that patriarchy obtains even in the characters' extreme and novel surroundings. In one representative scene we watch the three wives, stony faces streaked with dirt, huddled together in a row passing a tin cup of water among themselves, and we hear Thomas Gately tell the other men, "The going is easy, in these parts. We should make the most of this ground while we can"—to which Meek responds with a pessimistic comment. Although *all* the would-be settlers are at the mercy of Meek and nature, Reichardt highlights the women's unique alienation, their particularly grievous experience of having others control their fate. Repeatedly, deliberations about the journey take place among men, leaving the women without a say. But it would be wrong to describe Reichardt's heroines as passive. And, in fact, one way of understanding the growth in her filmmaking is to see the various ways in which her female characters appropriate the traditionally masculine and phallic symbol that is the gun. Whereas Cozy shoots and (apparently) kills at the end of *River of Grass*, *Meek's Cutoff* undermines traditional filmic gunplay. The only character in this film who fires a gun is a woman, Williams's Emily, and when she does fire, it's as communication, a warning shot in the air.

But of all the genre tropes that the film overturns, *Meek's* most directly subverts the *pacing* of the western. When Emily fires her rifle, Reichardt takes what would typically be a fast, dynamic, and rapidly edited sequence and slows it down. We watch every second of Emily loading the gun, firing it, reloading it, and firing it again, her heavy breathing and exasperated grunting registering the laborious process. This slow, unspectacular sequence indicates Reichardt's interest in time itself. Indeed, many of Reichardt's anticlimactic scenes could be explained through celebrated Hungarian filmmaker Béla Tarr's claim that, because nothing happens in his films, "all that remains is time" (as quoted in Jaffe, 16).[33] But these are complex remains. Reichardt's films invoke not just time, but a host of specific, associated phenomena: pace, momentum, and mobility; repetition and the experience of being lost; spending time with others; killing time (both the act of killing time and the kind of time that kills); "task time"; and boredom that shades into anxiety, dread, or grief. To address the sociopolitical stakes of Reichardt's temporal focus and filmic slowness more generally, we begin with a look at the "slow cinema" debates occasioned by her revisionist western. We then move on to consider the implications of slow cinema for the western—a genre with a particularly teleological sensibility. Whether triumphalist or mournful, this genre typically memorializes the past as a building block for the contemporary moment. Through pacing and a story that question the very notion of progress, however, Reichardt emphasizes the noninevitability of western settlement. Indeed, by reminding viewers that time's passage need not entail progress, narrative or otherwise, Reichardt shows that, for some, western settlement was not a story of victory but one long emergency.

The pacing and plotting of all Reichardt's films have led critics and scholars to associate her with "slow cinema"—what Jonathan Romney recently defined as "the varied strain of austere minimalist cinema that has thrived internationally over the past ten years" (43).[34] Some have even dubbed her "America's foremost practitioner of slow cinema" (Brady). Film scholar Ira Jaffe's recent *Slow Movies* offers a comprehensive definition of slow cinema that is worth quoting at length:

> To varying degrees, [slow cinema] movies are slow by virtue of their visual style, narrative structure and thematic content and the demeanor of their characters. With respect to visual style, the camera often remains unusually still in these films, and when it moves . . . it generally moves quite slowly. . . . Furthermore, editing or cutting in slow movies tends to be infrequent, which inhibits spatiotemporal leaps and disruptions. Not only do long takes predominate, but long shots frequently prevail over close-ups. Consistent with these stylistic elements . . . is the austere mise-en-scène: slow movies shun elaborate and dynamic decor, lighting and colour. Moreover, the main characters in these movies usually lack emotional, or at least expressive, range and mobility. . . . Further . . . the plot and dialogue in slow movies often gravitate towards stillness . . . and tend, in any case, to be minimal, indeterminate and unresolved. Complaints that "nothing is happening", prompted earlier in history by films directed by Antonioni, Andy Warhol

> and Chantal Akerman, paintings by Mark Rothko and Barnett Newman, and plays by Anton Chekhov and Samuel Beckett, arise anew regarding . . . [contemporary] slow movies. (3)[35]

Reichardt's films fit Jaffe's definition on almost all counts. The only exception we might take is that she employs tracking shots frequently—but her tracking shots are notably slow, to the point of causing discomfort or suggesting surveillance. We also should add that, like other slow cinema films, Reichardt's deploy an additional stylistic trait not mentioned in Jaffe's list: a tendency to favor diegetic over nondiegetic sound. Through this catalog of features, slow cinema thematizes time itself and makes it "palpable" or "visible"—in contrast to contemporary productions from both Hollywood and independent sources that usually subordinate it to other concerns: action, emotion, character psychology, and so forth.

Upon its release, *Meek's Cutoff* became a flashpoint for debates over slow cinema.[36] Describing his experience with the film, *New York Times* writer Dan Kois disclosed, "I had trouble staying planted in my seat with my attention focused on the screen, as the long dissolves from one wind-blasted plateau to another sent my thoughts blowing in a dozen directions." Focused on his own filmgoing experience, Kois does not seem particularly interested in the boredom of *characters*—and, therefore, the real-life people they may represent—even despite the fact that it is the monotony of these onscreen lives that typically informs the pace of the narratives, as in the case of *Meek's Cutoff*'s settlers' tedious, arduous journey across the arid U.S. West. When critics and bloggers such as Kois *do* shift from analysis of spectatorial experiences and positions to those of slow cinema characters, they tend to draw rather facile links between the former and the latter. As Kois tells us, "By the end [of *Meek's*], I could sympathize with the settlers' exhaustion; I felt as if I'd been through a similarly grueling experience." Kois's description of his boredom as a kind of labor, though probably intended as a joke, erases the specificity of Reichardt's depiction. That is, he erases the fact that her characters do a very different kind of labor, suffer a very different kind of boredom, and thus occupy a very different structural position from viewers.

Even when framed more positively, appraisals of slow cinema have still tended to fixate on the viewer's experience. Media and cultural studies scholar Nick Salvato declares that Reichardt's films exemplify "the experience of time moving slowly in a good, generative, and pleasurable, rather than boring or frustrating, way" (99)—but his declaration clearly does not hold true for the characters in her films (to say nothing of the debatable nature of this declaration, as Kois attests). Though Salvato later admits to the "excruciat[ing]" (118) experiences of *Wendy and Lucy*'s protagonist, he ultimately takes Reichardt's cinema as an opportunity to reflect on academic labor and to propose a slowing down of the pace of scholarly work: "the residual good feeling that may persist after having felt slow(ed) time can . . . encourage or buoy the scholar who then has to return to what for many feels comparatively like drudgery in the otherwise slow time spent at the archive or in the stacks" (123). The labor of Reichardt's *characters* is again erased, while questionable parallels are drawn between character and audience.

Salvato's discussion also exemplifies how terms such as *observation*, *meditation*, *appreciation*, *contemplation*, and *pleasure* recur throughout positive appraisals of the slow cinema movement. Indeed, for many critics, slow movies seem to lead to happy epiphanies, in ways that seem overly simplistic and therefore problematic. Film critic Edward Guthmann, for instance, observes that slow cinema icon Theo Angelopoulos's *Eternity in a Day* (1998) "seem[s] to whisper to us, 'Slow down, observe. Listen,'" and film critic and prominent Reichardt champion A. O. Scott avers that "In [the] wandering [that slow cinema invites] there can be revelation as you *meditate, . . . bliss out, luxuriate* in your thoughts" (our emphasis). These sentiments find perhaps their most succinct expression in blogger Harry Tuttle's proposal that slow cinema be referred to as "contemporary *contemplative* cinema." Such commentary posits slow cinema as a kind of pastoral for the present moment, a respite from our technologically saturated, nature-alienated, Hollywood-blockbuster-centered era. (Indeed, many scholars take for granted "the condition of technological, economic, and cultural speed-up that characterizes daily life in the twenty-first century" [Kendall, 113]—a commonplace that we trouble just below.) Such framing is particularly odd when one considers that films like *Meek's*, *Old Joy*, and *Wendy and Lucy*—and Semih Kaplanoğlu's *Bal* [*Honey*], Angelopoulos's *Eternity in a Day*, and Apichatpong Weerasethakul's *Uncle Boonmee Who Can Recal His Past Lives*, which critics have grouped with Reichardt's films—depict natural and other kinds of landscapes as haunted, sometimes literally, by questions of labor, loss, injustice, degradation, decline, and unrest.[37] Likewise, Scott's phrase, "*luxuriate* in your thoughts," again obscures the questions of economic and environmental struggle at the heart of Reichardt's and others' films. Although such pro-slow cinema commentators do avoid the facile suggestion that, say, watching a movie about settlers struggling to move west is *like* struggling to move west, they are no different in their disregard for the negative experiences to be found on the slow cinema screen.

The characterization of slow cinema as respite from contemporary modernity fails to comprehend that *slowness may in fact be a problem*, and a *problem of contemporary modernity* at that. Consider film scholar Jaffe's musing that "As *both* the spectators of such [slow] movies *and* the fictive characters who appear in them *sidestep the frenzy of modernity*, a slow, perhaps mythical past is invoked and a future more contemplative than the present is envisioned" (6, emphasis ours). But Reichardt and many of her slow cinema colleagues show how, for those on the fringes of society, modernity is actually experienced as slowness, and usually to their great detriment. In other words, Reichardt and other slow cinema filmmakers might be said to engage with the concept that postcolonial ecocritic Rob Nixon dubs "slow violence": "a violence of delayed destruction that is dispersed across time and space . . . violence that is typically not viewed as violence at all" (2). When Wendy borrows a cell phone in *Wendy and Lucy*, for example, it is not because she is, say, undertaking a technology cleanse, but because she doesn't have the money, or the stable address, to maintain a reliable one. And the would-be settlers of *Meek's Cutoff* are in the desert because they have become lost in their pursuit of a better life, not because they need a break from the hustle and bustle of city living. For both sets of characters, a slow drift out of secure economic conditions constitutes their "delayed destruction." Jaffe's active phrase, "*sidestep* the frenzy of modernity," imagines an agency that few, if any, of Reichardt's characters possess—and it mistakenly paints those who live slow lives as rested and content. Even though the pace of contemporary Western entertainment, communication, and consumption may be faster than in the past, the oppressive slowness depicted in a Reichardt film is equally a product of this fast contemporary era. Her films, that is, show the various and unequal temporalities experienced by people in the same era through their focus on those who get left behind in the "frenzy" of modernity; who experience the fallout of speediness as a sickening slowness.[38] These films thereby capture media and cultural studies scholar Lutz Koepnick's general concept of "cotemporality": that we "live in multiple times and spatial orders at once, in competing temporal frameworks where time often seems to push and pull in various directions simultaneously" (3) as well as Sarah Sharma's more pointed observation that "time is worked on and differentially experienced at the intersections of inequity" (as quoted in Salvato, 120). Rather than offering a mental vacation, Reichardt's slow cinema invites audiences to linger in a world where they might see ugly and troubling things, not (just) beautiful and soothing things.

The slowing down of slow cinema thereby enables audiences to see those things and people they might otherwise miss—not to "appreciate" them, but to ask what forces have encouraged this overlooking in the first place; to register invisibility and invisibilization as well as the invisible. A growing number of critics and scholars have recently come to similar conclusions—thus troubling the aforementioned readings and their depoliticizing tendencies. For example, Tiago de Luca and Nuno Barradas Jorge's 2016 collection *Slow Cinema* takes up film scholar and blogger Matthew Flanagan's claim that much of slow cinema attends "to marginal peoples (lowpaid manual labourers, poor farmers, the unemployed and dispossessed, petty criminals and drug addicts) subsisting in remote or *invisible* places, and depict the performance of (waged or unwaged) agricultural and manufacturing work that is *increasingly obscured* by the macro volatility of finance-capital's huge speculative flows'" (13, our emphasis); the collection features sections such as "The Ethics and Politics of Slow Cinema" and "Slow Cinema and Labour." In an essay in that collection cited earlier, Elena Gorfinkel speaks specifically about the political dimensions of Reichardt's work, seeing her "austere slowness [as] an aesthetic responsive to the harsh economic and ideological realities of the United State[s]" in the twenty-first century ("Exhausted Drift," 124).[39] Meanwhile, film scholar Karl Schoonover has clarified the dominant political values that undergird slow cinema by referring to its characters as "wastrels." The term "designates both people who waste [time] too easily and those vagabonds who society treats as waste and who, *like refuse*, are thrown to the side of the road" (68, our emphasis).

In addition to the double meanings of the term that Schoonover offers, we also can say that Reichardt's films, in their repeated tendency to diffuse climactic moments, also *refuse* certain traditional forms of pacing.[40] The emergencies Reichardt explores in *Meek's Cutoff* and *Wendy and Lucy* are characterized by suffering that often goes unnoticed because it is, in Nixon's terms, "attritional but also exponential," with "the conditions for sustaining life becom[ing] increasingly but gradually degraded" (3). In this way, Reichardt's slow cinema answers the major question that frames Nixon's work on slow violence: "how can we convert into *image and narrative* the[se] disasters that are *slow moving* and *long in the making*, disasters that are anonymous and star nobody, disasters that are . . . of indifferent interest to the sensation-driven technologies of our image-world?" (3, our emphasis).[41] By decoupling temporal progress from ideas of success and productivity and instead connecting time's passage to the slow unfolding of emergencies, Reichardt questions the teleological assumption that people in the United States are always moving toward a better future.

Meek's Cutoff takes up the question of time's relationship to historical progress by considering both the geographical and the existential side of having lost one's bearings. Indeed, Paul Dano's character carves the word "LOST" into a fallen tree just a minute and a half into the film. Whether metaphorical or actual, being lost powerfully illustrates the emergent quality of emergency. Unlike a dramatic catastrophe such as a shooting or an explosion, being lost requires the passage of time; is a *matter* of time. That is, one does not usually become lost immediately. And the bad possibilities of being lost do not usually take effect immediately, as with a shooting or an explosion. One becomes lost only after one has gone too far, or for too long, to easily find the way back. And being lost becomes a problem only gradually, as day cycles into night or summer cycles into winter, as light recedes, as temperatures drop, as supplies run out. Opining to her husband about Meek, their unreliable guide, Emily Tetherow uses the language of duration to describe the seriousness of their situation. "Two weeks he said we'd be in the pass; it's been five." Time spent *is* the crisis at the center of *Meek's Cutoff*: a promised better future seems to be moving into a farther, perhaps unreachable, time-scape as well as landscape. When Emily asks her husband whether the men have resolved to hang Meek or not, Solomon reports that the men decided "we'd give a few more days." In this way, the film's time-scape echoes its barren landscape, an unchanging expanse without markers of progress by which the characters might bestow meaning on their journey—or, more important, recognize where they are. The "few more days" Emily's husband says the settlers will wait out this emergency is the kind of lie people tell themselves when they are out of control of their lives. But even the amount of time that is to pass remains vague (a "few" days) because Mr. Tetherow knows that without Meek the settlers will lose all hope. If the hope they place in Meek is misguided, it at least organizes their traversal of a landscape without markers, a time-scape without events.

Even Meek, the film's unreliable and unruly cowboy, registers discomfort with undifferentiated temporal experience. Around the twenty-minute mark, Reichardt offers a medium long shot of him, and a distinctive bit of landscape—desert mountains—appears visible behind his shoulder. Reichardt then cuts to a tracking shot of the wagons, moving away from this landmark, and then back to a shot of Meek looking back at the mountains, trying to judge how far they've come and, thus, how far they have to go. One cannot look off into the distance and observe where the characters have been and ponder where they might go. The unvarying desert landscape with its whipping winds creates an overall sense that the characters' efforts and existence on the Oregon Trail will be erased, quickly covered over. After a particularly low moment for the characters—after they have discovered a lake and found it to be alkaline—Thomas constructs a marker of sticks, a fragile monument to the settler's presence that one imagines will not survive the brutal environment.

Like the "Goner" graffiti in *Wendy and Lucy*, Thomas's marker suggests the kind of historical counternarrative that Reichardt is interested in pursuing: These are the stories of those left out of, left behind by, and unremarked upon in tales of U.S. progress. Though *Meek's* is a period film, its commentary on U.S. hopes for better futures makes it an allegory for the present moment as well. Gorfinkel, for example, has suggested that by "[r]educing the scale of the actual expeditions of hundreds of groups," Reichardt's stripped down account achieves a "Beckett-inflected scenario of absurdity, bound by waiting, opacity, and non-knowledge" ("Exhausted Drift," 126). The modern resonance of such a hopeful pilgrimage is strengthened intertextually by Michelle Williams's recurrence as a woman on a failed road trip; in both *Wendy and Lucy* and *Meek's Cutoff*, she plays a character who, drawn by the promise of a better life out West, finds herself stranded. In addition, Reichardt reminds viewers not just of the losers on the way to our contemporary moment but also that the tools of modernity do not in fact guarantee progress—further chipping away at the idea that historical progress entails movement toward a better future. Like many westerns, *Meek's Cutoff* draws attention to the technologies of settlement. But like many other Reichardt films, *Meek's Cutoff* draws attention to technology's potential to break down. In addition to the tense climax centered on the (failed) lowering of wagons with a pulley leverage system, other scenes focus on coffee to be ground, shotguns to be loaded, sewing implements to be deployed, and axles to be mended—the latter, not unlike the broken serpentine belt that plagues *Wendy and Lucy*'s protagonist. (These transport components are even attended to by the same actor in both films, Will Patton.) Emily Tetherow explicitly invokes the specter of technology as she mends the Native American captive's moccasin; as if the silent man had just commented on her work, she suddenly declares, "This is nothing. You can't imagine the things we've done, the cities we've built." Seemingly an ethnocentric declaration of white achievement, this comment plays ironically against the dire situation in which the settlers find themselves, at the mercy of other people, fate, and nature. The fact that, in this shot, the bodies of Emily Tetherow and the Native American man are positioned together for the first time further undermines her commentary. Despite the narrative of technological advancement she invokes, Emily is in the same position as the Native American man. And the situation in which the settlers find themselves makes Emily's comment seem like a desperate attempt at shoring up belief in a historical progress that will include her—not unlike Wendy's insistence that she's going to make it to Alaska, or Emily's own husband's insistence that "this will all be a bad dream soon." The settlers are at many moments in a predicament similar to Wendy's, hoping that their transportation and other technologies will hold out just long enough to get them where they're going. They trust—they *must*—in narratives of progress, of certainty. But we see that their lives are in fact defined by diminishment, unpredictability, making that trust look more like the cruel optimism of Wendy in *Wendy and Lucy*. Whether documenting an uncelebrated past or a troubled present, Reichardt's films spend time with the losers of history. Indeed, it's not difficult to imagine some future viewer of *Wendy and Lucy* seeing Wendy's predicament in much the same way we consider the settlers': both are pursuers of an American dream who got lost along the way.

Meek's experiments with framing and visual style buttress this feeling of time passing without bringing progress. Reichardt shot the film using a 4:3 aspect ratio that makes for a relatively limited square view—in direct defiance of the post-1950s Western convention of using panoramic or otherwise wide shots to indicate open space and limitless horizons.[42] The latter convention, of course, invokes the belief in the plentitude, opportunity, and expansionism of Manifest Destiny. Perhaps it is not surprising that the strange shape of *Meek's* frame has disturbed contemporary film viewers. In her interview with Reichardt, *Fresh Air* host Terry Gross explains that, when she first began to watch the film, she thought there was a mistake in the way it was being projected. Because of the expansive vistas to which viewers, particularly viewers of westerns, have become accustomed, the 4:3 ratio feels like a denial, an impingement on visual freedom. In addition to boxy shots, Reichardt also frequently shoots low to the ground in *Meek's Cutoff*, preventing the sweeping views of "vast deserts and empty skies" (Wright, 12) for which the westerns of John Ford (*The Searchers*, 1956; *Cheyenne Autumn*, 1964), Howard Hawks (*The Big Sky*, 1952; *Red River*, 1948), Anthony Mann (*Cimarron*, 1931), and others are well known. Instead, when we do see the sky in *Meek's*, it is through claustrophobic shots of the punishing sun directly overhead. Reichardt has stated in interviews that this 4:3 ratio aligns the viewers with the characters because it "changes *time*. It keeps you in the present, where the characters are" (Buscombe and Fuller, 42)—producing the kind of shot in which "you wouldn't see tomorrow or yesterday" (Reichardt, as quoted in Longworth). Further limiting our perspective, Reichardt regularly places obstacles in our field of vision, even if minutely. The first three shots, for instance, are taken from behind blades of grass and branches—in much the same way that Reichardt shoots from behind foliage in works such as *Wendy and Lucy* and her short film *Ode*. In *Meek's*, these obstacles are filmed so closely that they appear at first as nondiegetic blurs on the screen.

Reichardt's stylistic refusal of the western's typical visual cues creates a visual and dramatic irony that, as in *Wendy and Lucy*, reveals both the precariousness of our protagonists and the cruel optimism that grips them. First is the obvious, but crucial, point that these protagonists cannot "see" *Meek's* cinematography. They are boxed in for us as viewers in a way that gestures toward their literal entrapment—but because, in the film world, they are privy to more expansive views, they can at least occasionally mistake their position as one of mobility and possibility. Indeed, though all the female characters wear blinderlike sunbonnets—surely also a commentary on the group's entrapment—they still can pan to the right and left, taking in the landscape in ways that we as viewers cannot. Only we can see that claustrophobic view, that writing on the wall, and it does not look good. The dramatic irony here is rather complex, then: in showing us less, Reichardt actually allows us as viewers to know more. These stylistic choices express the dread experienced by most of Reichardt's characters: They remain relentlessly in the moment, plodding slowly forward, though concerned about what the future might bring.

Even when Reichardt renders the landscape beautiful, she does so in ways clearly marked as not appreciable by her characters. For example,

Figure 8: Overlapping moments in *Meek's Cutoff* |

one of the film's most lovely moments features a lap dissolve, a transition that seemingly suspends the wagon train in the sky as Reichardt moves from one scene to the next. The wagons' traversal of the sky eventually crystallizes into an image of a further day of travel as the mountains come into view. This is one of Reichardt's few images of the West as open, expansive, and abundant. Because it is also the only image portrayed through a showy editing style, however, it also is clear that the view is available only to spectators, not the film's characters. Reflecting upon this distinction, we might say that Reichardt encourages her audiences to remember that what they are enjoying as an aesthetic experience also is a visualization of one moment blending into the next, the kind of undifferentiated time crushing the film's protagonists.

Trying to reject this feeling of suspension in an undifferentiated *now*, the characters try to meaningfully shape time as it passes. Meek's performance as a wise and knowing guide echoes Kurt's philosopher-stoner avoidance of the reality of his situation; in campfire scenes in both *Meek's* and *Old Joy*, men who are lost, literally and metaphorically in each case, attempt to stave off despair by bragging about their unique ways of knowing the world. Throughout the film Meek doles out his wisdom through certain favorite phrasings, one of which begins, "Hell is full of." Over the course of the film, making a "story to tell" out of his past experiences, Meek will alternately describe hell as full of bears, Indians, and mountains. But Reichardt's film revises Meek's account of hell. The cracked desert landscape, the constant fear of water running out, and the repeated patterns of daily struggle all create a hell of sameness, not a hell punctuated with eventful battles, as Meek would have it. Hell, in other words, is repetition. Indeed, the later image of the settlers carefully lowering wagons down a hill, only to see one split apart at the bottom, lends a Sisyphean overlay to their ordeal.

This Sisyphean view also appears in Reichardt's short films about loss. For example, *Ode*, her forty-eight-minute narrative short from 1999, announces the suicide of the protagonist's boyfriend within the first two minutes. The film thus starts at the end and wends its way back again, never allowing the viewer out of the circle that inevitably finds the young man dead each and every time. *Travis* (2004), which consists of color patterns and audio loops excerpted from an NPR interview with a bereaved mother of a soldier, describes grief as iterative. As the mother's ragged voice repeats, Reichardt slowly folds in novel phrases, starting with "Oh my God" and eventually ending with "I know that [at that] moment you said, 'I was shot momma. I'm so sorry. I know I promised.'" In this way, meaning builds through accretion; the audience's experience of the mother's anguish intensifies both from the duration of the process and the way that new focal points of pain continuously emerge. Although another Iraq War film might put the son at the center, or might lead up to the tragic event of the IED explosion, this one refuses viewers the kind of cathartic release that clear climaxes offer. *Travis* thus theorizes through abstract image and sound what Reichardt reveals through concrete image and plot in her narrative films: The time of emergency is simultaneously cyclical and durative, repetitive, even as it stretches oppressively forward.

Throughout Reichardt's films, characters' negative experiences with surplus time clarify the stakes of slow cinema's plotting by revealing a class-specific experience of boredom. In *River of Grass*, *Old Joy*, *Wendy and Lucy*, *Meek's Cutoff*, and, to a lesser extent, *Night Moves*, we find figures needing to kill time, figures waiting. But with the prominent exception of *River of Grass*, they are not waiting for something *interesting* to happen, as might be the case of narratives focused on more privileged characters.[43] Instead, Reichardt's characters are waiting for something *critical* to happen: for mobility to be regained (or lost); for rights to be granted (or taken away); for freedom, or just one's next paycheck or meal, to be secured (or slip out of reach). Reichardt's characters passively wait for those critical happenings; their boredom is not the mundane boredom or melodramatic ennui experienced by the privileged. Instead, in Reichardt's films, characters attempt to pass time in ways ranging from Cozy and Lee's foolish antics in *River of Grass* to the deadly serious prayers that form the first audible dialogue in *Meek's Cutoff*.[44] Even the seeming indolence of characters such as Cozy and Kurt serves to show the link between killing time and the reduced agency of the down-and-out, as Reichardt depicts the boredom that arises when one has little control over the world in which one exists.[45]

The way characters pass their days in Reichardt's film worlds testifies not just to their boredom, but also to what might initially appear to be more productive uses of time. Beginning with its title card, *Meek's Cutoff*

Figure 9: Reframing the western in *Meek's Cutoff* |

highlights what might be called "task time." The film opens on an image of a hand-embroidered rendition of the film's title. In our interview with her, Reichardt explained that all her films, but especially *Meek's*, focus on chores: "*Meek's* is about the labor it takes to walk across the country and the chores involved." Lattimer has suggested that although "the various iconographical markers of the Western in the film immediately evoke a sense of familiarity in the viewer, the continual emphasis on the chores that allow this Western world to function represents a clear break with the traditional, more event-driven demands of the genre" (40). More particularly, the film shifts the focus to the labor of women that has largely been erased from the historical record. An exemplary scene quite literally reframes the western through the time of women's labor. After discovering that the lake they have come upon is alkaline, the men ride off on horseback. Unlike a traditional western, *Meek's* lingers with the women; Reichardt frames the iconic western shot of the men riding off into the distance with the women doing laundry in the foreground, shifting the focus to the uneventful task time of women's chores.

In the context of the characters' hopeless situation, Reichardt's emphasis on task time serves an additional function. Through her depiction of repetitive tasks, Reichardt shows the way that a day's chores become laden with near talismanic meaning for those unready to admit how lost they are, or how undifferentiated their experience of time is at risk of becoming. In *Meek's Cutoff*, the women's attempts to keep a home life going out on the Oregon salt flats indexes their dogged commitment to maintaining indicators of the better life they hope to achieve. The first time Reichardt shows the campsite, we see that the families have created three distinct "households," each with its set of chores and upkeep to be maintained. In a later scene, three separate campfires light the morning darkness as the women rise to cook meals for their families and start the day. Ironically, however, these very actions that mimic a more successful life may in and of themselves be depleting. In the harsh world of the Oregon desert, the attempts to maintain private households begin to seem insane, as one wonders about the wastefulness of the three separate campfires and the labor involved in brewing three pots of coffee—signs of the better life that appears to be passing out of the settlers' reach. Such attempts to retain the privatized and respectable domesticity of life back East echo the daily routines Wendy establishes around her new life in the broken-down car. Although it's not entirely unfair for viewers to complain that "nothing happens" in a Reichardt film (or any other slow-cinema film), we might consider that, in their depictions of characters trying to make events out of "nothing," her films recalibrate what constitutes an event. Through their daily habits and rituals, Reichardt's characters attempt to ward off the despair that would entail giving up any attempt to manage time's passing and losing all sense of or hope for progress. Put more bleakly, her films show the way happenings that would be nonevents for those doing well in life are in fact life-changing emergencies for those in precarious socioeconomic positions and the way seemingly banal chores become freighted with meaning in those emergency states.

A scene depicting the decimation of the domestic respectability Emily has worked so hard to maintain literalizes *Meek's* interest in splitting apart time's passage from notions of progress. When Emily tosses her family's possessions from the back of her wagon in an effort to lighten the group's load, Solomon briefly considers a pendulum clock—an arbiter, of course, of duration. "That was my mother's," he remarks. Emily responds, "I know." As her husband describes the transformation the object has undergone—"it's only weight now"—Emily heaves it into the wasted landscape. Although Solomon likely cares deeply for his mother, Reichardt does not tell us anything about their relationship, or anything about Solomon individually, that would allow us to imbue the clock with special meaning. Instead, we can only imagine that Solomon's care for his possessions has equal "weight" with anyone's care for his or her own objects. At the same time, the clock's reduction from family heirloom to mere mass helps viewers grasp the truly dire situation of the settlers. An heirloom is a promise of survival, of continuance. Emily and Solomon's grim, efficient disposal of the clock then not only suggests their bad fate, but how they are stuck in a bad present moment: ties to the past (mother) and future (children who might inherit an heirloom) cannot matter now.

As Reichardt's plots move along, the characters seem decreasingly likely to escape their situations. This stuckness in time is heightened by other narrative, visual, and sonic techniques that work to emphasize duration's tightening noose. In *River of Grass*, for instance, Reichardt uses the bullet-ridden intertitles to mark the number of days Cozy and Lee have been hiding out; in *Old Joy*, the film begins with striking gongs that continue as the film progresses; in *Wendy and Lucy*, Wendy's notebook tracks her dwindling money against the dates that keep on ticking forward; and in *Meek's Cutoff*, the settlers measure their days on the Oregon Trail against their own diminishing supplies, just as the real-life women who inspired these characters marked their days in diaries. *Then, a Year*, Reichardt's short film centered on the aftermath of crime, lingers on the images of a wristwatch left in the woods and a kitchen timer that has run its cycle, the hand back at zero. These films thereby illustrate Bonnie Honig's observation that "survival's needs reduce us, they make us focus on specifics, immediacies, the needs of mere life" (10) as well as Gorfinkel's concept of "enduration," "persisting through forms of duress" ("Weariness," 318). In each of these films, then, but most dramatically in *Meek's Cutoff*, Reichardt shows the way that *time kills*—how it reduces one, to use Honig's terms—at the same time that her characters *kill time*. Time becomes a measure not, say, of how much one has grown or how much one has accomplished, but, rather, one's ability to endure in the face of diminishing chances for survival.

Even Reichardt's titles invoke the weighing of time: *Old Joy*, *Then, a Year*, *Ode*, and *Night Moves* each refer to a sense of time that slips away, a kind of pastness or belatedness.[46] And though time that slips away is seemingly at odds with time that must be killed, or that kills, Reichardt shows that time's ability to be simultaneously boring and too fast in its passing are two sides of the same coin, particularly for people living through emergencies. We see this most acutely in *Wendy and Lucy* and *Meek's Cutoff*. In these films, although time may drag slowly, it also moves relentlessly forward, indifferent to the fact that the characters' resources cannot outlast its passing. Reichardt's narrative and formal choices dovetail in this regard: her feature films contain no flashbacks or flash-forwards, tend to favor restricted narration, and eschew subplots and crosscutting (with the exception of *River of Grass*).[47]

As suggested by the slow-cinema debates *Meek's Cutoff* occasioned, by the time the film reaches its climax some audience members may feel as desperate for a change as the characters. But the nature of the film's crisis point reveals Reichardt's ironic engagement with traditional modes of plotting emergency states. On Emily's assurance that there will be water over a ridge, the settlers engage in a painstaking procedure of lowering their covered wagons down a ravine through a system of ropes anchored by their bodies and winched around a rock. This sequence takes place largely without dialogue and in the absence of music; instead, as in the bomb-building scene in *Night Moves*, the heavy breathing of the men and women holding the ropes and the squeaking of wagon tires score the scene.[48] As they lower the third wagon, the rope snaps—producing the fastest motion in the film. Finally, we have "action." But as the wagon comes to its shattering end, Reichardt's camera comes in close to show how banal the measure of true devastation can be: the water barrel, thrown from the wreckage, rolls, opens, and slowly releases its meager contents into the desert floor. Though this fast-moving explosion is dramatic, horrible, it isn't the real crisis here; the settlers can share the other two wagons, and they eventually do. They cannot, however, exist without water. This is both a crisis that has been coming since the film's beginning and one that will pay its dividends in similarly incremental amounts. Even in a climactic moment, the threat in a Reichardt film is always of a slow decline or death.

In the aftermath of the wagon's wreck, Reichardt shows the way that people press on in the face of emergency—because they must—and the way some people come to realize that to endure such crises may require different ways of relating. When Meek spies the Indian sifting through the wreckage of the Tetherows' wagon, the former approaches aggressively, shouting, and draws his gun. Registering the Indian's fearful response, Meek taunts, "so you got some feeling in you after all." Though this taunt shows Meek's sense of the Indian as subhuman (as though he might *not* have feelings), Meek's threatening behavior toward a living member of the party, no matter how much of an outsider the Indian may be, causes Emily to draw her own weapon. Meek responds by invoking the unknown as threat: "you people got no idea what you're dealing with here." "Neither do you, Mr. Meek. You've proved that amply by now" replies Emily. Whereas for Meek, the indefinite future is reason enough to kill, for Emily and Solomon it's a reason to band together. Through the conflict between the cowboy, the Indian, and the white woman, Reichardt repurposes the western showdown to explore how one reacts to spending time with difficult figures, particularly in states of emergency.

Although relating is hard in Reichardt's worlds, as we have seen in *Wendy and Lucy*, we are interested here in the particular way that time stresses relationships. Because her films focus on very few characters overall, and because they eschew subplots and crosscutting, viewers receive little respite from unlikable or frustrating characters. Moreover, because Reichardt refuses to provide backstories or clear motivations for these characters' actions, their bad decisions cannot be explained or excused—say, because of past trauma or some other sympathy-inducing factor—and, therefore, their opacity is further frustrating. And, after *River of Grass*, we rarely see Reichardt's characters doing anything quirky, spectacular, shocking, or otherwise nonbanal that would at least make these flawed figures unique or interesting. (Indeed, while *Night Moves*'s protagonists may build a bomb, theirs is perhaps the least exciting bomb-building sequence in cinematic history.) Finally, these characters come together with others in ways that specifically highlight time. Put another way, time spent watching a Reichardt film is time spent watching characters spend time together, whether it's *River of Grass*'s Cozy goofing around with Lee in a hotel room as they wait to get caught, or Mark and Kurt and the settlers on their silent and lengthy treks in *Old Joy* and *Meek's Cutoff*.

Moreover, because Reichardt frequently focuses on trying characters in trying situations, she encourages us to reflect on our own ability to stay in the moment—a moment in which we may be tempted to abandon the lives depicted on screen. *This*, then, is the shared experience of viewers and characters: not (necessarily) labor or boredom, as Kois, Jaffe, and others would have it, but exploring the limits of one's empathy. Take, for example, the moment in *Old Joy* when Mark has entirely lost patience with Kurt. After their night camping, Kurt puts an optimistic spin on the extension of their trip when they sit down at a diner: "This is better anyway, no rush, we can take our time." But when the waitress comes to take their order, Mark's frustration with his friend becomes clear. "Need more time?" she asks. "Nope!" comes Mark's quick response, a negation of Kurt's embrace of their newfound "quality time." In the context of being together as a phenomenon of time, Mark's brusque rejection of "more time" also is his rejection of Kurt's friendship. Such exploration is, as Reichardt has it, fundamentally temporal: the capacity to spend time, to *invest* time, in others. Without characters with whom we can easily emotionally bond, and without events to entertain us, we must find new strategies for building relationships and different modes of attention. These strategies include ecological thinking, as we discuss in our next section. Indeed, Reichardt's focus on scarcity and precarity, coupled with her interest in (often failed) relationships, reminds us of how ethical responses are shaped, if not *determined*, by available resources, both material and immaterial, natural and manmade. As Reichardt asks, are care and compassion—*and time for others*—in short supply as well?

Reichardt also has created a notable interpersonal dynamic in every single one of her films to date: She offers at least one character who is slightly more of an outsider—more down-and-out, more flaky or unreliable or on the fringe—than her already-outsider characters. The latter characters find themselves, usually to their chagrin, obligated to spend time with the former. In *River of Grass*, Lee is this person to Cozy; in *Old Joy*, it is Kurt to Mark; in *Wendy and Lucy*, the crust punks to

Wendy; in *Meek's Cutoff*, Meek and the Native American man alternately to the rest of the settlers; and in *Night Moves*, a nameless man to the main crew of three. This recurring interpersonal dynamic, we argue, matters on multiple levels. One, it highlights the downward mobility of Reichardt's protagonists: how they start near, but not at, the bottom, before spiraling further down. Two, it speaks to the socioeconomic dynamic that Reichardt invoked in our interview when discussing the dubious pleasures of the contemporary U.S. reality television show *Teen Mom* and the bad life decisions it showcases: In each film's case, there is another figure that one can point to as being worse off or as making worse decisions, thus allowing characters and film viewers alike to feel self-congratulatory about their—our—comparatively good decisions. In forcing her characters, and us as viewers, to spend time with these outliers, Reichardt counters not only the American Dream vision of upward mobility, but, more generally, the sense of superiority that often informs refusals to extend empathy: *I would never allow myself to wind up in that position.* To use the language of economics, what we often see depicted in Reichardt's films, then, are people who *spend* time with one another but fail to *invest* in one another.

Of course, one might argue that there is good reason to avoid such connections. As we have already discussed, connections may *cost* something, whether it be Kurt mooching off Mark or the crust punks in *Wendy and Lucy* who seem genuinely threatening. The Indian represents this ambiguity most clearly: The settlers have no way of knowing whether he is a helpful or harmful figure. Moreover, letting the Indian live means the settlers must weigh the potential that the Indian knows where water is against their need to give him their own precious water. The potential costs of caring for a stranger unfold over the course of scenes that find the settlers in very different places with their resources. Upon Solomon and Meek's arrival with the Indian, the matter of whether to kill the captive is up for debate. Later, when a woman's scream pierces the dark silence of a night scene, Emily emerges from her tent to see the settlers crowded around the Native American man, trying to interpret the rocks he has been painting. "It's his religion," Solomon suggests. "It's signals," Thomas insists. Meek, for his part, takes the debate over the rock paintings as an opportunity to renew his case for lynching the man. But Solomon returns to his mantra of waiting, arguing "things'll look better in the light of day." And though Thomas challenges him, "This is on your head, Solomon," Tetherow only repeats his message of patience: "It's fine, give it another day." In this moment, two responses to spending time with the discomfiting stranger appear to be offered. Meek's call to kill "the Indian" marks the extreme edge of the desire to put an end to time spent with an unknowable and difficult other. In contrast, Solomon's plea for patience, if not exactly an expression of concern for the other, at least refuses a quick dismissal, deferring the judgment of him for another day. Later, when Emily brings the man water, Meek, who has been observing the scene, teases her. "How's your friend?" he shouts. Emily responds, "About the same as us; tired, hungry." Where Meek's question means to imply difference—the fundamental incompatibility and unbridgeable distance between the English-speaking white woman and the Nez Perce–speaking Native man—Emily's response accounts for their shared experience in time and space. Indeed, the Indian's dialogue is never translated, leaving him as unknowable to most viewers as he is to the characters. In this way, Reichardt's focus on emergency reveals shared positionality, if not shared feelings. In the desert of *Meek's Cutoff*, all depend on a dwindling, precious resource—female and male, white and Native American, human and nonhuman.

When the film ends, we do not know how the relationship between the settlers and the Indian will turn out. Screenwriter Raymond sees the abrupt, opaque ending of *Meek's* as a happy one in this sense: "by my reckoning, the question has been answered: at least for now, they're not killing him. They are making a leap of faith toward nonviolence, for better or worse. They are accepting the limitations of their knowledge and choosing to trust someone they wouldn't otherwise trust" (Colford). But the visual style of the film remains highly ambiguous. The last set of shots begins with Emily's face framed through clearly visible branches; then the Indian framed with the same branches in the shot's foreground, as if from Emily's point of view; then a return to Emily's face still obscured by the branches. In the very last shot, we cut back to the Native man. This time, rather than being closely framed through branches, he appears in a full, open shot, and we can see for the first time the plains on which he stands, the hills behind the plain, and a strip of sky beyond that before the film fades to black and ends. The irony, of course, is that although this open, final shot contrasts the tight shots we have just seen, it does not point toward any definite freedom from need, any particular deliverance from crisis. The ending's ambiguity is only heightened by the knowledge that its abruptness is due in part to Reichardt's own problem with resources—funding ran out, making it impossible to shoot one final scripted scene (Gorfinkel, "Exhausted Drift," 134). The film's haunting last image, then, is a double testament to continuance's always indeterminate and provisional nature.

It is in this visually expansive and yet uncertain ending that *Meek's Cutoff* parts ways with other films that have likewise been dubbed revisionist westerns, such as *The Wild Bunch* (dir. Sam Peckinpah, 1969), *Dances with Wolves* (dir. Kevin Costner, 1990), and *Dead Man* (dir. Jim Jarmusch, 1995). Those films, like *Meek's*, are critical of U.S. "progress" and expansionism, but they nonetheless treat white settlement as inevitable. But *Meek's* is different. This visual-spatial openness that Reichardt does afford us at the end, is, paradoxically, suffused with dread and uncertainty. Just before the final set of shots, Emily Tetherow declares, "We're close." Thomas Gately responds, "That's just it. We're close. But we don't know what to." As *Meek's Cutoff* ends, it is possible that the Native American will lead the settlers to water, but it seems just as likely that death waits around the corner. Reichardt's settlers are not just lost; they may turn out to be the losers of history. Ending the film as she does, Reichardt suggests the contingency of U.S. history and thereby refuses to naturalize the story of white civilization's triumph. Reichardt's ongoing questioning of concepts of progress, both narrative and historical, continues in her next film, *Night Moves*. Though focused on Oregon of the twenty-first century, this next film finds the white settlers of the area still in a water crisis—an intertextual irony that suggests Americans have progressed very little indeed.

Environment: *Night Moves*

In the water-scarce 1845 Oregon of Reichardt's *Meek's Cutoff*, rogue guide Stephen Meek tells would-be settler Thomas Gately, "The beaver [has been] played out. . . . That market's done and gone. [But] there are plenty of fortunes to be had. The beaver's just the first gift of this land." Set in present-day Oregon, Reichardt's subsequent film *Night Moves* shows inhabitants still struggling with water-related conflicts.

And it offers a very different account of the gifts of the land, one that resonates ironically with Meek's prophecy and highlights Reichardt's interest in emergency as a long, slow process. The 2013 film depicts environmental activists Josh, Dena, and Harmon blowing up a dam and then what follows in the wake of their actions, including the accidental death of a bystander. In a tense scene preceding the bomb's placement, Dena states that "by 2048 the oceans are gonna be empty." "We should go fishing sometime before it's all gone," Harmon replies. Separated by two hundred years, 1845 and 2048, the absent beavers and fish testify to the precarity of life. But whereas Meek treats the beavers' disappearance with nonchalance, Josh, Dena, and Harmon are all too aware of mounting species loss.

We should note that Reichardt's favored shooting location and setting in itself gestures toward environmental crisis. The Pacific Northwest is known at least as much for battles over limited natural resources and fragile ecosystems—including the Northern Spotted Owl debates and the Pacific timber battles of the 1980s and 1990s that resulted in the Northwest Forest Plan in 1994—as for those resources and ecosystems themselves. And Oregon also has been the site of a number of famous "ecoterrorism" cases, to the extent that two special bills were introduced to the state legislature in 2013 to enhance punishment against radical environmentalist activism.[49] More specifically, the area has been the site of what we might call an environmental culture war, with environmentalists and working-class citizens positioned on either side of a widening chasm. One aspect of this war was memorably captured by 1990s bumper stickers ranging from "Save the Spotted Owl" (the species whose survival was being threatened by logging) to "Kill a Spotted Owl—Save a Logger," and by President George H. Bush's declaration that Senator Al Gore was "so far off in the environmental extreme that we'll be up to our neck in owls and out of work for every American" (Devroy). In this war, environmentalists were framed, perhaps unfairly, as elite and un-American, but also, perhaps fairly, as ignorant of how their demands might affect local communities. Meanwhile, working-class citizens were posited, sometimes unfairly, as wantonly careless about nature and as nestled so deeply in the pockets of big business that they could not recognize their own vulnerability. What is notable about Reichardt's cinema, in this broader context, is not just how it tracks the Pacific

Northwest's history of environmental exploitation, but how cognizant it remains of class issues as it does so, refusing to pit working-class whites against environmentalists and showing the complicated allegiances that bedevil both sides.

But although environmental concerns subtend all of Reichardt's Oregon films—from garbage in the forest in *Old Joy* to the references to the shuttered lumber mill in *Wendy and Lucy*—*Night Moves* makes these concerns explicit. As we show in this section, Reichardt's generic shift from western with *Meek's* to thriller with *Night Moves* is crucial to her class-conscious environmental commentary. The thriller's emphasis on hidden schemes, convoluted plans, conspiracy, surveillance, and recording, and its moods of paranoia and dread, match the environmentalists' machinations and its ensuing fallout. But Reichardt employs these elements to emphasize, paradoxically, both human complicity in environmental crisis and the complex interconnections that make it difficult to place blame. We claim that she plays, more specifically, off the so-called paranoid thrillers that had their heyday in the 1970s, in keeping with an era marked by the corruption and secrecy of the Nixon administration. In films such as *The Manchurian Candidate* (dir. John Frankenheimer, 1962), *The Conversation* (dir. Francis Ford Coppola, 1974), *Chinatown* (dir. Roman Polanski, 1974), the original *Night Moves* (dir. Arthur Penn, 1975), *All the President's Men* (dir. Alan J. Pakula, 1976), and *Blow Out* (dir. Brian De Palma, 1981), an underlying system of control, usually in the form of a complex conspiracy, is revealed by the end. In Reichardt's *Night Moves*, however, no specific conspiratorial network ultimately materializes. In obviating this typical cathartic moment, Reichardt points to the stubborn facts of environmental crisis: There are too many players; too many victims who are also perpetrators; underlying causes that are too big and too abstract to swing at, or perhaps even to comprehend, from capitalism to the surveillance state.

Or, put more sinisterly, *Night Moves* emphasizes the way everyone is connected, the way consequences and blame for current environmental conditions are dispersed, as in a network. For example, prior to Dena's prediction of empty oceans, Josh makes his own comment about the precarious existence of fish in the Pacific Northwest when justifying the violent act the trio are about to undertake: humans are "Killing all the salmon just so you can run your fucking iPod every second of your life." However misguided, the plan to blow up the dam is Josh's attempt to make people see they have nonhuman deaths on their hands. "It's gotta be big. People are gonna start thinking. They have to," Josh tells Harmon. Part of Reichardt's project, then, is to showcase more and less misguided attempts to render networks of environmental harm and degradation visible, using the thriller genre to bring the hidden connections between, say, salmon decline and iPods, to light.

Such attempts are difficult because of the frequent imperceptibility of environmental harm and degradation, how they easily fade into the background of everyday life—at least in the relatively privileged West. In an early scene, Josh walks through a grove on the organic farm where he works. As he looks toward the camera, his face framed by trees, a sound bridge layers itself on top of the sound of chirping birds: "the disaster we see is happening everywhere at the same time. The clock is ticking." And yet, we *don't* actually see it happening, at least not in this idyllic setting. Reichardt then cuts from Josh to a scene of makeshift film projection. Isolated, sometimes apocalyptic, images of nature and wildlife flicker on a white sheet in front of a row of heads. The female voice, which we soon realize belongs to a documentary filmmaker presenting at this environmentally minded gathering, continues,

> It has been ticking for one hundred and fifty years now, since the dawn of industrialization. We are a culture hooked on profit, production, and perpetual growth. But at what cost? The disaster is happening to our farmlands, it is happening to our oceans, our forests, our wildlife. It is happening to our climate. How long will it be before humanity understands that everything is interconnected? How long till multinational corporations understand that they can't make a profit off a dead planet? So let the revolution begin, all around the globe. An army of individual citizens must rise up and take a stand. For the future, for the people, and for the planet.

During the hostile question and answer session that follows, attendees demand to know what solution the documentarian has in mind. Reichardt turns her camera to Josh's hard, cynical face, as the filmmaker responds, "I'm not focused on big plans, I'm focused on small plans. A lot of small plans." But Josh, as noted above, is focused on big plans. In the next scene, he and fellow malcontent Dena purchase a boat that they, along with their coconspirator Harmon, will pack with explosives and use to bomb a dam that they see as representative of environmental harm.

The documentary sequence punctures idyllic visions of nature to point to a nature that is degraded and *being degraded* at a sickeningly slow rate ("ticking for one hundred and fifty years"), much as Reichardt's human protagonists slowly sink further and further into bad situations. The trio's reactionary plan, then, is not just a big one but also a *fast* one: They attempt to combat slow and invisible violence through a swift and spectacular act. Here, Reichardt's interest in duration takes on a distinctly environmental dimension. Although, as we have argued, contemporary Western life is routinely characterized as fast-paced, that characterization fails to make sense of the slow violence of environmental degradation (not to mention the experience of marginalized humans). In arguing that Reichardt's films are about those places and persons who get left behind in, or suffer from, the "frenzy" of modern life, and who experience the fallout of rapidity as a sickening slowness, our view departs from that of many ecocinema scholars—on much the same grounds as those on which we depart from many "slow cinema" scholars in our discussion of *Meek's*. Scott MacDonald, for example, in considering filmmakers such as Peter Hutton (Reichardt's Bard College colleague), has complained that "going to the movies . . . increasingly means an acceleration in our rates of consumption: both the implicit consumption of more and more images and sounds per minute and the literal consumption of amounts of food and drink." MacDonald therefore sees "the fundamental job of an ecocinema as a retraining of perception, as a way of offering an alternative to conventional media spectatorship, or . . . as a way of providing something like a garden—an 'Edenic' respite from conventional consumerism—within the machine of modern life" (109). We are optimistic that Reichardt's œuvre—which we are here considering as a kind of ecocinema—could retrain perception, and we are certain that it constitutes "an alternative to conventional media spectatorship," but we are arguing that it offers *not* a respite from modern life nor a chance to contemplate some kind of pure nature, but an opportunity to recognize the slow violence that is environmental degradation under modernity. In this context, when Josh, Dena, and Harmon craft a fast plan—or when Harmon, speaking of the boat, slyly comments, "If I was keeping her I'd say there are some repairs to do. [But] I guess we don't give a shit about longevity, do we?"—we must understand these moments as desperate attempts to, first, change their, and the environment's, status quo, and second, to mimic the strategies of the powers that be. After all, it's the British Petroleums of the world, not the environmental activists, who typically "don't give a shit about longevity."[50]

Like *Meek's Cutoff* before it, *Night Moves* invokes not just environmental problems in general, but in particular the management of that precious resource, water. The film opens on a shot of a large industrial spout that suddenly starts spraying a massive blast of water—an image that, juxtaposed with the mortal thirst in *Meek's*, looks positively obscene. (A reverse shot of Josh in contemplation suggests this valve as part of the dam the group will later target.) A few scenes later, when Dena ducks into a home improvement store to obtain fertilizer for bomb making, she walks past a bubbling water feature; Reichardt's camera stays trained on this object after Dena has left the foreground and even the whole frame altogether. When Dena and Josh check out their prospective boat, the camera swoops across the interior of the seller's house, revealing through the windows an artificial waterfall in the man's backyard. And when Dena and Josh first meet up with Harmon, he engages them in a diatribe about the sprawl of the "Portland empire," demanding, "Guess how many golf courses there are in Bend already?" "Five," Josh ventures. "Fifteen," says Dena. "Twenty-nine!" Harmon bellows, almost amused by the absurdity. "It's the high plains desert. Where's the water!?" Tallying these scenes, *Night Moves* starts to feel like the *Chinatown* of slow cinema. But although water is being identified as new grounds for unprecedented global conflict,[51] Reichardt focuses on the unwitting yet wasteful abuse of a vital resource in the most undramatic and benign of settings. As always, Reichardt points to emergency's everyday manifestations.

It is important, then, that *Night Moves* shows how its protagonists, would-be environmental heroes intent on bringing important truths to the light of day, are themselves implicated in environmental crisis. Reichardt therefore keeps with the theme of the compromised hero found in many thrillers, but she goes beyond it to show characters whom we might even describe as part of the conspiracy they oppose. The trio despises capitalism and the idle rich, though the bombing of the dam is (unknowingly) financed by Dena's wealthy father. And Harmon actually works at the golf courses he criticizes. When he admits he has not yet acquired enough fertilizer, and Josh becomes irritated, Harmon rejoins, "I have to work. Those greens don't mow themselves. You know?" We might therefore read these figures as hypocrites, but a more important point inheres: In an economy, and world, in which one can find little work that is restorative and fulfilling rather than draining or destructive, it often seems as if the only option is to blow the whole thing up.

Night Moves thus offers a slightly different version of "the system" than that on view in *Old Joy* and *Wendy and Lucy*. When the home improvement store clerk insists on seeing Dena's social security card before he will sell her fertilizer, it may initially remind the viewer of the security guard's sympathetic lament to our protagonist in *Wendy and Lucy*: "You can't get an address without an address. You can't get a job without a job. It's all fixed"—except, in this situation, Wendy is contemplating her attempts to secure gainful employment, not destroy public infrastructure. But what we have in both instances are people who are immobilized; people who can't escape the system; people who can't redeem themselves even if they tried. We might in fact think of Josh, Harmon, and Dena as one possible alternate version of Wendy—Wendy after realizing that working at the cannery won't get her ahead in life, or that she can never get to the cannery in the first place—or younger versions of *Certain Women*'s late-middle-aged construction worker, who is too poor to retire but too disabled to work; out of desperation, he enters his former employer's headquarters and takes a hostage. These individuals give up on trying to follow the rules of the system, although, of course, they ultimately still find themselves stuck. Here, again, Reichardt challenges us to look at characters and *not* ask, "What were you thinking? What did you think would happen?"—the refrain that routinely greets bad decisions. She creates worlds of diminishment, whether economic or environmental or both, in which the horizon of a good future is so inconceivable, and the slow march toward decline so unbearable, that a desperate, disruptive act, whether shoplifting or bombing or taking hostages, looks like a decent choice indeed. If nothing else, it promises a change of pace.

Even screenwriter Jon Raymond, presumably more mobile than Kurt, Wendy, or the *Night Moves* trio, admits his embeddedness in the system. In response to questions about how he happened upon the source material for *Meek's Cutoff*, he recalls that

> Back in 2007 or so I got a freelance job as a "namer" for some fancy branding company in Portland. At the time, the city of Bend, Oregon, was growing at an insane rate, and the developers were hiring people to give their new properties a patina of prestige by fashioning them as somehow predistressed. Anyway, I got a gig naming a golf course out there, and in the historical research for that I came across the story of Stephen Meek, a mountain man who was famous mostly for leading a wagon train around in circles in the high plains desert. (personal communication)

Although the political (and environmental) dimensions of an "insane [growth] rate" can be inferred through Harmon's commentary in *Night Moves*, Raymond makes the broader political implications of his screenwriting work explicit in speaking of *Meek's Cutoff*: "The pioneers on that voyage weren't sure whether their guide was evil or stupid and took regular votes on whether to lynch him or not. In the middle of the Bush era, this model of botched leadership and a riven community seemed incredibly germane" (personal communication). Perhaps it's no surprise, then, that Raymond has a rather wry view of his own participation in the system. Responding to an interview question about the arguably inconclusive end of *Meek's Cutoff*, Raymond declared, "What happens next is on a certain level obvious: these people, or people like them, make it to Oregon; the Indians are decimated; a hundred fifty years later some yuppie asshole like myself names a golf course after them" (Colford). What becomes clear in Raymond's self-aware discussion, and in Reichardt's positioning of Harmon, Dena, and Josh's protest as contaminated by the very systems they wish to destroy, is the way in which environmental crises are rhizomatic, giving the thrillerlike feeling of a conspiracy in which corruption spreads in a dispersed fashion, but with no central root of evil to be easily located and eradicated.

Although the paranoid thriller thus seems to be both Reichardt's biggest influence and her biggest counterpoint, she has pointed to other genres and even other media forms as influences. In our interview with her, conducted during the final stages of editing *Night Moves*, she cited her affinity with U.S. landscape artists such as painter Charles Burchfield (1893–1967) and photographer Joel Sternfeld (b. 1944). To understand the overlap between the thriller and landscape art for Reichardt, we might consider the importance of surveying and surveillance to each genre. Thrillers are characterized by conspiracies and convoluted plans, but they also are about observational mastery, often featuring technological control over sensory fields, as seen in films as diverse as *Vertigo* (dir. Alfred Hitchcock, 1958), Penn's *Night Moves*, and *The Net* (dir. Irwin Winkler, 1995).[52] Surveillance in thrillers and surveying in landscape art are both modes of trying to uncover the truth of a particular environment.

But Reichardt's influences reject the expansive, straightforwardly Romantic landscapes offered by U.S. painters of the Hudson River School and their disciples. They engage, instead, with landscapes that resist surveillance and refuse to offer up their secrets to a masterful human gaze. For example, Charles Burchfield habitually includes power lines as structuring elements in his paintings and places sharply diagonal tree branches in the foreground of his images—not unlike the way Reichardt shoots from behind leaves and branches and puts power lines front and center in works like *Then, a Year*.[53] Skepticism toward humanist and Romantic views of landscape also characterizes the work of Joel Sternfeld, a contemporary photographer whom Reichardt called a "really 'American'" artist in our interview. In each of the fifty images collected in his book *On This Site: Landscape in Memoriam* (1997), Sternfeld captures places where acts of violence and crime have taken place, long after the fact, such as the Grandy's restaurant where, in 1991, Wanda Holloway paid a man to kill the mother of her daughter's cheerleading rival.[54] In addition to sites of *brutal* violence (intended, if not realized), Sternfeld also depicts sites of environmental and economic disaster—sites of *slow* violence. A photograph titled *Hanford Reservation, Hanford, Washington, August 1994*, for example, refers to the land on which the United States built its first large nuclear reactor and dumped more than 440 billion gallons of nuclear waste (Sternfeld n.p.), which has had long-term negative health effects on local residents and workers. In contrast to the massive scale of this disaster, the photograph captures a prosaic image of heaped soil in the foreground, industrial equipment in the background against the skyline, and a billboard advertisement reading, "It's the nature of our business" in the middle of the frame. Without titles and explanatory captions, one might not know that Sternfeld's photographs are not merely portraits of frequently ugly U.S. landscapes. In this way, Sternfeld shares Reichardt's concern with the imperceptible and the slowly emerging.

Reichardt's connection to landscape art makes further sense when we consider that *Night Moves* shows *both* humans and environments under intense surveillance, often at the same time—whereas, of course, the thriller focuses solely on humans. Thus, although all Reichardt's films could be described as bearing a tone of dread—as in, for example, the many tracking shots of the vulnerable Wendy in *Wendy and Lucy*—in *Night Moves* this tone extends beyond human characters and also becomes overtly thematized. For example, when Dena goes into the store to try to purchase fertilizer, Harmon warns her that there are "cameras on the edges of the store. Stick to the center aisle." Despite this warning, we are led to believe that she does get recorded; when Dena speaks to the store manager (James LeGros) about the quantity of fertilizer she's buying, Reichardt shows a video camera mounted high in a corner of the ceiling. In this same room, an aerial photograph of farmland hangs on the wall behind the manager's desk, suggesting more elaborate technologies of surveillance. Recording technology, we learn, has even reached the campground from which the group embarks on their voyage to the dam. As Harmon warns Josh, "careful where you park, the lot has cameras now." Harmon even jokingly imagines a nature so suffused with surveillance that it itself becomes a spy; when Dena and Josh first arrive at his woodland trailer, he teases, "Let's get back inside, okay? There's narcs everywhere out here. And the raccoons are not to be trusted."

The universality of surveillance, even in supposedly natural environs, suggests its paradoxical implications: although the cameras in the campground might be there to ensure its preservation as a pristine site, their very presence changes the environment they are meant to maintain. Ecocritic David Mazel, in his work on biosurveillance, captures this paradox:

> [I]t is not merely that we moderns know more about nature, but that . . . we behold nature in a particular way: as the object of [a] sort of panoptic gaze. . . . Our perspective has been decisively shaped by *global biosurveillance*, a term I use to denote the vast and growing complex of activities that *enable us, first, to understand living nature as a biological whole*—as the biosphere—and, *second, to strip it of layer after layer of what used to be spoken of as its "mystery" (and thereby render it increasingly amenable to human ends)*. (186, latter two sets of italics ours)

Reichardt, in *Night Moves* and elsewhere, clearly engages with such concerns, but some important differences inhere. First, in her vision of biopolitics, there is no monolithic category of humans—"*we moderns*"—to which she opposes nature. As we have suggested, Reichardt's œuvre reminds us that different humans have different experiences of modernity. A second, and related, point is that many of Reichardt's human characters find *themselves*, right alongside nonhuman entities, living under biosurveillance. Put another way, surveillance is part of the everyday experience of all life. But we might therefore read the presence of cameras in the campgrounds ironically: the powers that be, we can assume, have used crime as a pretext to "emergencize" (Del Savio and Mameli) the everyday, just as global terrorism has inspired the securitization and militarization of everyday life, from airport body scanners to Facebook check-ins after disasters. After all, as the *Night Moves* trio's concern indicates, what the cameras likely militate against is not environmental degradation but, rather, efforts (like theirs) that oppose it. Such emergencization occludes the fact that everyday life, as Reichardt shows us, is *already* an emergency.

Again, *Night Moves* is concerned not just with surveillance but also with *recording*. Here, we see why the thriller, at least in its most basic form, works well to articulate environmental degradation. Thrillers such as Coppola's *The Conversation* and Michael Haneke's *Caché* (2005) focus on recording, on proof, but environmental degradation is similarly a matter of the record, of proof—of evidence of what humans have done in and to the environment over time. We might think, for instance, of environmentalists' frequent recourse to comparative graphs and statistics, as seen in films such as *An Inconvenient Truth* (dir. Davis Guggenheim, 2006). And indeed, environmental conversations have of late turned to the concept of the Anthropocene, the notion that humans have so changed the geologic record that we need a new name for the current era.[55] Thus, we might say that Reichardt maps environmental change as a record of human intervention onto the thriller's traditional focus on recording technologies. More specifically, she shows how unintended consequences go on the record, whether a criminal or a geologic one. Midway through the film, for example, the three protagonists gather for breakfast and discuss how to purchase fertilizer for their bomb.

Reichardt shoots them framed by a mural on the wall behind them, depicting an idealized vision of westward expansion complete with train station, rosy skies, and all the signs of a newly built town. Reichardt thus brings together an image of the planning and settlement that created the environmental conditions our protagonists wish to reverse with an image of their own planning. In both instances, the humans in question are oblivious to the unexpected negative consequences of their planning. Both groups, the settlers in the painting and the activists in the foreground, are trying to change the landscape, though of course in different ways. The unexpected irony, clearly not considered in the frenzy of optimism rendered in the mural, is that it turns out you can't change it back.

A conversation between Dena and Harmon during the mural scene suggests this bind: after a busboy recognizes and greets Harmon, he explains that they served time together in prison. When his compatriots seem unsettled, he insists it was "so long ago, it doesn't really count. It's gone, expunged." Outraged at his casual attitude, Dena demands, "You think your record is gone? You think anything is gone anymore? . . . Nothing is ever gone anymore." With this line, Dena also makes plain the major departure of *Night Moves* from the thriller genre. In other thrillers, finding oneself under surveillance is a special occurrence, a

Figure 10: A mural of Western progress in *Night Moves*

shocking revelation, a function of the rare and riveting experience of being caught in a conspiracy. But *Night Moves* makes surveillance a ubiquitous, everyday, and thus "normal" experience—just as anxiety and dread subtend everyday life in Reichardt's other films. *Night Moves* is thus perhaps the perfect film for an era in which massive surveillance and recording of U.S. citizens by the National Security Administration has been exposed—and, more important, in which the U.S. public responded to that revelation with apathy, lack of surprise, and even support.[56] Here, the larger ironies of Reichardt's filmography become clear: her thrillers aren't thrilling, and her "boring" movies, as discussed earlier, are in fact often quite terrifying.

After the boring uneventfulness of Reichardt's previous films, it's a bit surprising when something explodes; when the trio's bomb goes off. But *Night Moves* pointedly frames this explosion as being both too late and ineffectual. As the trio starts driving away from the scene, the bomb blast can be heard from offscreen, and Harmon chuckles as they keep driving in silence. After so much waiting on the part of the audience, Reichardt's choice not to show the explosion helps to show the way in which plans may not matter, a point that develops with increasingly high stakes from this point in the film forward. Indeed, the bomb explodes at minute 58 of the 112-minute film, after which the plot shifts and the rest of the film is taken up not with the environmental discussion they hoped their act would provoke, but with the fallout of an unintended consequence of their actions. When Josh reassures Dena, "we've just gotta get home, show up for work tomorrow morning, just get back to normal," we suspect this is unlikely, both from an environmentalist and from a genre perspective. But Josh is both wrong and right: on the one hand, *Night Moves* is a film about all the small ways in which things cannot be set right once they're in motion; on the other hand, *Night Moves* documents the difficulty of effecting change. The morning after the explosion, for example, Josh's employer, an organic farmer, registers his disgust with the "theater" of the explosion when he reads the news. He points out the purely symbolic nature of this action: "one dam, who cares. That river has like twelve dams on it. The grid is everywhere." The farmer's assessment, a paranoid statement apropos of the thriller, is also an accurately pessimistic account of the uphill battle faced by environmentalists. In this film about trying to conceal, erase, or reverse various track records, Reichardt's interest in duration takes a notably pessimistic turn.

Among all the characters in *Night Moves*, Josh is the most paranoid, and also the one who most tries to wrest control of biosurveillance operations. He attempts to avoid being put in the position of natural environments—those surveilled and exploited entities that he fights to defend. When Josh and Dena buy the motorboat that will become a floating bomb, for example, Josh asks the man selling the craft (named *Night Moves*) whether he can use the bathroom in his house. When he goes inside, we see him eyeing the house with great distaste, showing his habit of surveying the lives of others and also the judgmental side of his character. Later, he eavesdrops on Dena and Harmon having sex. And finally, he spies on and murders Dena, necessitating his flight out of town. But this would-be mastermind—who receives the most point-of-view shots in the film—also is quite vulnerable, a fact that Reichardt suggests throughout the film but particularly in its last scene. There, Josh walks toward an outdoor goods store from the parking lot. Reichardt's camera pans to follow him, suggesting a security camera's movement. Once he enters the store, Reichardt cuts to a close-up tracking shot from his point of view, passing several glass cases of merchandise. The products that fall under his gaze are binoculars and then hunting knives—once again tying surveillance to violence. But Josh isn't here to buy or even steal this equipment. Apparently trying to start over, he asks the staff about putting in an application. The manager asks him, "Are you from around here?"—a refiguring of Wendy's constant refrain, "I'm not from around here"—and "Do you have a car?"—something Wendy certainly does not. Josh replies in the affirmative to both. This dead-end retail gig at a corporate outpost could be the alternative career for a former organic farmhand, one that Wendy would be lucky to latch onto. But the film's last few shots imply that things will not go well for Josh. He stares at the blank application that imposingly demands data like his contact information and previous employment—data he cannot provide, just as Wendy has no address or telephone number to offer when filling out forms at the pound and jail. He looks up, and the film cuts to its last, sustained shot: a surveillance mirror that reflects everyone in the store. Josh, a watcher, is here the watched. The film thus ends on a markedly pessimistic note. Nothing has changed as a result of the bombing, cell phones are everywhere, subjects are still under surveillance, and, in filling out a job application, Josh continues to participate in systems of bureaucratic record keeping. The grid is indeed everywhere.

This same sense of diffuse and persuasive surveillance occurs in several iterations of the thriller genre, of course—such as Coppola's *The Conversation* and novels such as Paul Auster's *City of Glass* (1985). But it has a particular salience in Reichardt's work. Her particular stylistic patterns indicate that Josh, her most explicit "bad guy," might not be such an outlier in terms of her filmography. Specifically, the point-of-view tracking shot wherein Josh surveys binoculars and knives is not an isolated flourish but a structure found elsewhere in Reichardt's œuvre—most prominently in *Wendy and Lucy*, when our titular human character goes to the pound. Just as Josh moves past the glass cases on his right, scanning the merchandise, so does Wendy move down a hallway of kennels, scanning on her right to see whether her dog is inside. Both shots pay homage to *Umberto D.*, which contains a similar shot from inside a pound, as De Sica's protagonist looks for his dog. While Josh and Wendy and their respective predicaments may seem quite different, the parallel tracking shots remind viewers that both are living in bureaucratic and police states, surveillance states. And both employ the epistemologies of those states even as those epistemologies are simultaneously used against them. Both characters, moreover, find themselves in degraded positions marked by futile, belated activity. Wendy, putting aside the question of how she will care for herself, looks for the one for whom she cares. Josh, an environmentalist once so antiestablishment that he blew up a dam, now hopes for an entry-level job at a corporate outdoor-goods in a strip mall. Both have internalized not only the techniques of the surveillance state, but also the logic of the American dream. But neither, as Reichardt makes clear with their downwardly mobile trajectories, will save them.

Aftermath

Many of Kelly Reichardt's films begin in medias res or even later, after what most viewers would consider the major, or catalyzing, event has already taken place. She thus either cuts out what makes a climax *feel* like a climax—preceding events that serve to provide explanation or to build up tension—or cuts out the climax itself. This narrative tendency enables her focus on what we call aftermath: the often-banal, but no less painful, modes of living that follow from a crisis. Even when Reichardt's inspiration or referents are spectacular—Hurricane Katrina or the Iraq and Afghanistan wars—her films tell antispectacular, everyday stories. Consider, for example, Reichardt's *BOMB* magazine interview with fellow director Gus Van Sant, in which she alludes to a hypothetical backstory for *Wendy and Lucy*: "we imagined Wendy as a renter; no insurance, just making ends meet, and a fire occurs due to no fault of her own and she loses her place to live." Here, the fire provides the seeds of the story but remains well offscreen, the subsequent experience of homelessness instead forming the film's action. Similarly, though Reichardt's larger real-world inspiration, 2005's Katrina (Van Sant), had a spectacular moment as a storm, it was the widespread lack of infrastructure, the flooding, and the lingering dampness that made homes uninhabitable and life unbearable—causing structural elements to putrefy, mold to grow slowly, and diseases to fester. In other words, the example of Katrina shows the way disasters tend to hang around, continuing to distribute their effects.

In this way, Reichardt's "aftermath cinema" rejects the good-feeling closure and catharsis that traditional narrative arcs provide. But it has a potentially larger import as well. Bonnie Honig, for example, has critiqued the ways that philosophical and theoretical accounts of the place of emergency in democratic politics have tended "to focus attention on the moment of emergency and not on the afterlife of survival" (9). In what follows, we explore Reichardt's insistence on the aftermath and afterlife of emergencies—and propose that aftermath and afterlife *are* emergencies, by definition. In looking at her first five features and all three of her shorts, we call attention to the meanings embedded in emergency's shared root with "emerge": to "come forth," or "issue *from*."[57] In these readings, we consider how animals as well as humans in Reichardt's films experience what comes forth, or issues from—showing the broad extent of our filmmaker's interest in aftermath.

Wendy and Lucy exemplifies Reichardt's in medias res plotting. The film begins with Wendy already halfway to her Alaskan destination. And the most crucial fact of the film, that Wendy's car dies, is treated in an unspectacular manner. In fact, we would argue that this event should be understood as having already happened before the film's action even begins. It would then be more proper to say that Wendy's car *is dead* in *Wendy and Lucy*, rather than to say that it *dies*—a seemingly simple observation that has major ramifications for how we understand Wendy's position, as well as Reichardt's tendencies. To wit: the opening sequences of the film show Wendy playing fetch with Lucy; Wendy meeting a group of crust punks; Wendy going to sleep in her parked car; then Wendy being awakened by the security guard who asks her to move the car, at which time she finds it will not turn over. At no point do we see Wendy actually driving the car. Thus, although it's not made explicit, Reichardt encourages us to imagine Wendy's car as being fatally impaired even before the opening scenes of the film. And indeed, Wendy's interactions with a local mechanic locate her car trouble much earlier in time. When she first visits him, she reports, "a guy in Salt Lake City said that he thought [my serpentine belt] was cracked, and that it would probably run about $150 for a new one." When she returns late in the film to hear the results of the mechanic's inspection, he affirms this—"The guy was right about the serpentine belt. It's cracked all over the place. Just a matter of time before the car gave out on you"—but also informs her that her car has been afflicted by other, worse calamities: "But that's not why your car won't start. . . . You *snapped* a piston rod. Actually, you *blew* the head gasket *first*, water got into the cylinder, *probably when you cooled it down*. And the rod can't compress the fluid then. And there you go, *you ended up* with what they call 'Hydrolock'" (our emphasis).

The fact that Wendy did not repair the belt at the time speaks to the painstaking calculations and recalculations of time and money that those on the economic fringes must perform. But perhaps more important, the film offers another set of problems, events that not only took place in some general unspecified past, but that went unnoticed by Wendy. The car's death may have been spectacular on a small scale, what with its snappings and blowings, but those events were not visible to the naked eye or ear. And that small spectacle is only presented to Wendy, and us, indirectly, through a character's retroactive description. Thus, the film sets us up as viewers to focus on *aftermath*, while emphasizing Wendy's lack of agency when it comes to events that directly affect her. Indeed, what we've seen in the roughly 80 percent of the film that has transpired before the second scene with the mechanic is Wendy being forced to deal with the aftermath of a particular calamity, *regardless of whether* she can comprehend it. Such post hoc plotting and explanation further develops Reichardt's critique of neoliberalism's emphasis on individualist narratives of success and failure. Beginning in the after, that is, allows her to push against emphases on personal responsibility and self-efficacy. Arriving after the fact, like spectators at a crime scene, we see there's nothing Wendy can do at this point.

As in *Wendy and Lucy*, *Meek's Cutoff* begins with its protagonists already far into their journey. Where the former film depicts several days in Wendy's life after she has become stuck, the latter depicts several days in its protagonists' lives after they have become lost. Although *Meek's does* offer us a rather spectacular event in the form of the accidental destruction of one of the group's wagons—which contrasts with the silent, invisible, and unseen death of Wendy's car—the film makes it abundantly clear that the group was in dire straits long before the dramatic accident. The few other pieces of information we receive about the group's experiences strengthen our sense that critical events have already taken place, offscreen. For instance, when Stephen Meek comments on Emily Tetherow's relative youth, Solomon Tetherow testily responds that his first wife died. We also listen to Thomas Gately worry to Meek that the group has arrived in the territory too late, after its natural resources have already been depleted. Thus, even though the would-be settlers have arrived relatively early in terms of the western genre—the film is set in 1845, whereas westerns typically cover 1860 to 1890 (Wright, 5)—Reichardt stages the film as if they are quite late to the pioneering party.

In her short films, Reichardt follows a similar temporal and narratological orientation, beginning at, or even after, crises or major events. For example, in addition to *Ode*'s circular narrative structure discussed earlier, we also might note that the central character's suicide has already taken place in the larger cultural imagination—and, thus, the film technically starts after that event. *Ode* originally derives from the 1967 hit song by Bobbie Gentry, "Ode to Billie Joe," which was adapted into a novel and screenplay by Herman Raucher and then produced and directed for the screen by Max Baer Jr. in 1976, as *Ode to Billy Joe*. (Reichardt credits Raucher's novel as *Ode*'s source in the opening credits.) And indeed, Reichardt's version seems to anticipate, or at least encourage, viewers' familiarity with the song and its subsequent adaptations. For instance, when Bobbie Lee's mother announces, "Just got some news from Choctaw Ridge. Seems Billie Joe McAllister—seems the boy jumped off the Tallahatchie Bridge," she echoes Gentry's lyrics almost verbatim.[58] The stuttering awkwardness of the actress's announcement may stem from the fact that the lines have been changed so little that she is in essence reading what was intended to be sung, rhymes and all.

Following from the idea that emergencies are not localized, do not have a singular point of climax (or, at least, that that point is not the most important one), Reichardt denies the possibility of clean breaks in human relationships. Specifically, she often focuses on death and ensuing grief; even when one of the parties to the relationship is gone forever, things drag out as people try to come to terms with the severed bond. Both *Travis* and *Ode*, for instance, capture how traumatic events are experienced recursively rather than linearly, and how grief so often entails the mental and emotional replaying of loss. But whereas *Travis* performs that work through its nonnarrative experimental form and sound editing, *Ode* does so through its predominantly retrospective narrative structure and visual repetition. After the news of Billie Joe's death is delivered in its first few minutes, the film flashes back to the story of the relationship between the protagonist, Bobbie Lee, and her boyfriend, Billie Joe, and the events that apparently prompted his suicide. After the relationship and events have been outlined, Reichardt's *Ode* loops back to the present time and we watch the very same tripartite shot sequence featured in the beginning: Bobbie Lee's mother announcing Billie Joe's death; Bobbie Lee's grief-stricken face, captured with a zoom-in; and then Bobbie Lee wandering the woods in a daze. The sense of recursive trauma articulated by this repeated sequence is heightened by Reichardt's choice of *structural* repetition: after the tripartite shot sequence appears at the *beginning* of the film, *Ode* cuts to a shot of Billie Joe alive, which launches the flashback portion of the film; when the sequence appears again at the *end* of the film, *Ode* again cuts to a different shot of Billie Joe alive, which eventually turns into a freeze frame with which the film ends. In this way, Billie Joe "dies" twice in the film, and "lives" twice after the news of his death.

In addition to offering an incisive portrait of the operations of grief, the film tragically ironizes Bobbie Lee's adolescent tendency to replay events. For instance, after Billie Joe first kisses her, she goes home and reenacts the kiss with her pillow. Later, as she prepares for a meeting with him that seems to promise sex, the narrator states in a deadpan voice, "Bobbie Lee knew something was about to happen. Something magical. Something she would replay in her mind for years to come."[59] But the meeting in fact ends in his revelation of his homosexual desires, which in turn leads to his suicide. We as viewers already know that the latter is coming because the film starts with the mother's announcement. And, one could argue, the omniscient narrator knows it too—making his comment about "Something magical. Something she would replay in her mind for years to come" sound horrifyingly sardonic. The film's last line, the narrator's—"Did you know that somebody loved him?"—also is highly overdetermined. We know very well that someone loved him. And if she doesn't love him still, she will at least be "replay[ing] in her mind for years to come" his ultimate fate.

The fact that many viewers already know the tale of Billie Joe McAllister means that watching Reichardt's *Ode* will involve their own cycle of replaying. *Ode*, then, exists as part of the aftermath of the Billie Joe McAllister suicide, fictitious though it is (albeit resonant with many high-profile gay youth suicides of recent years):[60] The film offers itself as yet another artifact to be placed in this tragic incident's extensive archive. Thus, when the narrator declares in the film's final voiceover segment that "A boy was dead in the Tallahatchie River. You remember him. Billie Joe McAllister," viewers may hear this statement as "You remember him *from other iterations of the story*"—especially considering that it would be rather strange if we could not remember a major character in the film we've just watched.

The narrator's "You remember him" has further implications, though. Beyond serving as a description of our experience of the film—after learning of his death at the beginning, we "remember" Billie Joe through the film's extended flashback—it also can be heard as a prediction or even a directive to us as viewers: "You *will* remember him." The importance of remembering also is built into the retrospective narrative structure of Bobbie Gentry's original "Ode to Billie Joe."[61] Gentry stressed the importance of remembering in later interviews, suggesting that the real theme of the ambiguous song was indifference. In fact, its verses recount the nonchalant reactions of the narrator's family to the death of her erstwhile, clandestine boyfriend. Reichardt in turn highlights this indifference, with the protagonist's older brother musing, "If I was gonna jump, I'd [go to the] Hall Bridge." Against such indifference, *Ode*'s structural and referential cues to remember insist that viewers will not be so callous.

We have suggested earlier that the experimental style of *Travis*, which features shifting abstract images and looped found recordings, gives a record of grief's lasting nature. Also, it gives a picture of war in terms of its aftermath. Reichardt's choice to tell the story of the mother, rather than the soldier son, and to loop the mother's comments, adding and layering, registers war's true costs—costs that do not end with the end of a life on the battlefield. The film thereby gives the lie to terminology such as "surgical strike," a term the U.S. military has used throughout engagements in the Middle East since Desert Storm, which implies that war can be conducted through clean cuts that neatly cleave people from this earth. Reichardt here explores the messiness of war in terms of what happens after the explosion. We understand that the son's death has psychic effects on the mother that could go on forever, much like the constantly shifting and reorganizing phrases that make up the film. "Oh my god. Oh my god," the mother whispers. At another moment she seems to try to find meaning in her son's death, declaring, "I believe [the war] had to do with dollars and cents." These two phrases and seven others repeat in various combinations, none of which provide relief, a sense of meaning, or a place of rest. The sorrowful round Reichardt creates from the mother's grief has no logical endpoint, any more than war itself has logic. In this way, the mother's vocal tracks suggest that even when wars are not nuclear, their fallout follows a kind of Zeno's paradox of half-lives, never again arriving at a stable preemergency state.

Like *Travis*, Reichardt's fourteen-minute experimental film *Then, a Year* also engages with the aftermath of human heartbreak while absenting humans from the visual frame. Also like *Travis*, the film consists of images filmed in the nostalgic home-movie format of Super-8 and contemplative nondiegetic voice recordings—though, unlike in *Travis*, the images are not abstract. The majority of voice recordings in *Then, a Year* consist of reconstructions of love letters written by the infamous Mary Kay LeTourneau to her thirteen-year-old male student. Other bits of *Then, a Year*'s narration seem randomly drawn from true-crime television shows—which, as in *Ode*, typically begin with terrible events and then work back in time. Indeed, *Then, a Year*'s sound remains firmly focused on the retrospective, whether the byte emerges from narrator types—such as the *Dateline*-esque "And the only thing that would prove worse than the mystery was the truth"—or, somewhat more poignantly, from various apparent victims, survivors, and other bystanders: "He was definitely a chameleon. He could be this or that;" "Had he got the help he needed at the very beginning, this may never have happened;" "Should I have known better? I should have. I should have." Like the mother in *Travis* and Bobbie Lee in *Ode*, the speakers replay traumatic events in their minds, extending the experiential time frame of the event beyond the duration of the event itself. (We can imagine an older Bobbie Lee asking herself over and over why she couldn't have recognized earlier that something was wrong; how she could have been so self-indulgently preparing for her "first time" when her sweetheart was, meanwhile, preparing to end his life.) And in fact, the speakers often seem to be referring retrospectively to a time long before the crime, such as in "He was definitely a chameleon. He could be this or that."

Of course, some of these comments seem to voice regret and remorse rather than grief, per se. We can imagine, for example, that the person who refers to the "chameleon" has been duped, not bereaved. But they display the same impulse we see in Reichardt's work more broadly: to produce portraits of people who are somehow stuck. In the particular cases of *Ode, Then a Year*, and *Travis*, it is the past that provides the sticking place. Thus, an interesting dichotomy between Reichardt's features and her short films emerges: whereas in her feature films excruciating temporal experiences are lived out in the immediate—characters kill time while waiting to be arrested, characters wander day after day in search of water—in her short films, it is the retroactively oriented, ancillary experiences of grief, trauma, regret, and hindsight that stretch time out and make it unbearable. Although the replaying of terrible events might serve for some as a way to process them, it also can, Reichardt suggests, become its own hellish version of killing time.

Though the cause is less clear and less violent in *Old Joy*, the film's protagonists also find themselves managing the fallout of a relationship that has ended. The image from the film that best analogizes the wreckage of Kurt and Mark's friendship is that of their campsite. When they decide to stop for the night, Mark and Kurt settle on a campground turned dumpsite replete with an old couch that they sit on to drink beer. Raymond's original story further encourages us to consider the degraded setting's parallels to more everyday home life. When Mark and Kurt turn onto a logging road—an indicator, of course, of environmental modification—Raymond describes it as culminating in a "narrow *cul-de-sac*. . . . The headlights . . . settled to reveal an old love seat, some kitchen chairs, and a smattering of soiled papers and *carpet samples*" (*"Old Joy,"* 7, our emphasis). With an aged brocade couch, torn lampshade, and other household items on view, the campsite demonstrates environmental and economic degradation, but it also suggests the aftermath of a homey life that has fallen apart, leaving behind just this debris. The love seat and other wreckage visually echo the "bad" furniture and domestic unease of *River of Grass*, and their status as castoff trash might allow viewers to imagine them as the twenty-first-century parallels to the heirloom that Emily Tetherow throws from the back of her wagon in *Meek's Cutoff*. Though they constitute someone else's trash, these are items encrusted with a memory of a settled, warm domestic life. When

Figure 11: Gleaning women in *Meek's Cutoff* |

the travelers wake the next morning, after Kurt's drunken confession of feeling anxious about the status of their friendship, we see them picking through the campsite, trying to extract their own valuables—perhaps a metaphor for picking through the detritus of their relationship to see whether anything might be worthy of salvage.

Another term for picking through waste is, of course, gleaning. And gleaning, the practice rendered aesthetic by Jean-François Millet's 1857 painting *The Gleaners* and taken up in recent documentaries such as Agnès Varda's *The Gleaners and I* (2000) and Lucy Walker's *Waste Land* (2010), recurs throughout Reichardt's cinema. An allowance by which French gentry provided for peasants by permitting them to scavenge the fields after harvest time, gleaning permits survival by recycling what others discard as waste. In the Industrial Revolution's aftermath, Millet brought to his urban audiences an account of peasant life, which art critic John Berger describes through a catalog of labor, including "scything, sheep shearing, splitting wood, potato lifting, digging, shepherding, manuring, pruning" (70). As we have established—and as Reichardt discusses further in our interview with her—her films focus on "chores" or "tasks"; the necessary labor that must be continued, even under the harshest of conditions. But gleaning is unique among the chores Millet and Reichardt represent because of its dependence upon the waste of another class. In this way, we might consider gleaning a chore that takes place in states of aftermath—and, in Reichardt's films, it is a function of both economic and environmental degradation. That is, gleaning takes place after the best resources have been extracted from an environment; it is a strategy for making do with what has been left behind.

Reichardt's films engage with multiple accounts of gleaning. At the beginning of *Old Joy*, for instance, Kurt appears on the scene pulling a red wagon filled with cast-off items and cheerfully announces, "I borrowed a cooler . . . and a wagon, and a TV."[62] We see a more clearly local account of contemporary urban gleaning in *Wendy and Lucy*, when Wendy and the homeless individuals in Wilsonville, Oregon, collect aluminum cans cast off as trash, ostensibly by the wealthier members of the local community. Though we would not wish to validate the wasteful forms of consumption that produce excess trash, in such moments of urban gleaning we do see a practice of human adaptability and improvisation springing up in the wake of, and perhaps in spite of, the

Figure 12: Gleaning firewood in *Meek's Cutoff*

privileged classes' wasteful consumption. Recycling becomes recast, not as a top-down bourgeois lifestyle choice, as exemplified by San Francisco's mandatory composting law, but as a survival strategy for living in emergency that comes from the ground up.

Visual references to gleaning and its actual practices allow us to understand *Meek's Cutoff* not just as a western, as discussed earlier, but as a kind of postapocalyptic film. The costuming, color palettes, staging, and even the number of female characters in *Meek's Cutoff* echo Millet's famous *Gleaners* painting. As the second day within the film's story time opens, Reichardt frames the women coming through the field in a group, gathering sticks of firewood from the dried-out land; here, we might understand them as taking up the eighteenth-century strategy for dealing with what is left behind. If the settlers are indeed seeking a "new Eden" out West, then we must imagine that they have been cast out of the original Eden—perhaps for their wasteful destruction of it. Though Emily tells the Native American man that he "can't imagine what we've done, the cities we've built," her claim on civilization also must be weighed against Meek's noting the dwindling resources in the West. By these lights, the pilgrims' shrinking water supply and the saline lake they encounter allegorize a world in which consumption levels threaten to be outpaced by the rate at which the earth is degraded and poisoned. What has happened to the wonderful cities back East, we might wonder? Where has the clean water gone?

In this sense, we might see *Meek's Cutoff* as an aftermath film in two particular, related ways. First, it is a film of environmental crisis. Second, it is a film of the Anthropocene—or a work of "Anthropocinema."[63] What is unusual, of course, is that the film is set in the mid-1800s. Most films focused on environmental crisis or the Anthropocene—for example, Richard Fleischer's *Soylent Green* (1973), Godfrey Reggio's *Qatsi* trilogy (1982–2002), and Joon-ho Bong's *Snowpiercer* (2013), or even Reichardt's own *Night Moves*—tend to be set in the future or some version of the present, thus suggesting that scarcity, degradation, and pollution are impending or recent phenomena. Such films thereby make such phenomena feel shocking rather than mundane, and they do little or nothing to explain how we got to our current moment of crisis. In depicting the mid-nineteenth-century United States—famously, a moment of (at least belief in) plentitude and spoils—as already degraded, Reichardt suggests both a longer genealogy and a slower pace of emergence for environmental crisis. *Meek's Cutoff* thus nicely illustrates the claim made in her later film *Night Moves*, that "the clock has been ticking" for some time now—thereby framing the entire period of modernity as one big, drawn-out emergency.

At another point in *Meek's Cutoff*, Reichardt again uses the concept of gleaning to show the ways that people continue to make do in, and after, crisis—while also suggesting that crisis should inspire a reevaluation of inflexible judgments about ownership and use rights. As the settlers sort through the wreckage after the wagon-lowering disaster, Meek begins to shout at the Native American man: "put that down! That don't belong to you!" The man is handling a woven basket, part of the Tetherows' wasted domestic space. Emily replies, "What does it matter, leave him be." Meek replies, "It's the principle of the matter." This exchange, echoing the rigid moralism of *Wendy and Lucy*'s stock boy ("If you can't afford dog food then you shouldn't have a dog"), suggests both the ignorance and the cruelty, whether intended or not, of "principled" stands in emergencies and aftermaths. This is also the moment that leads to Meek and Emily's standoff, as he trains his gun on the gleaning Native American and Emily responds with her own threat of violence, holding her rifle on Meek. Though Emily's message—"What does it matter"—is ultimately nihilistic, Reichardt's focus on gleaning practices illustrates the ingenuity, and the shifts in values, brought on by life in aftermath.

Reichardt's concern for life-in-the-after extends beyond her human characters. We have suggested earlier that nonhuman animals are key to Reichardt's attempts to stress the banal, everyday suffering of marginal people—how the drive to provide not just for oneself but for dependent others like pets entails waiting; suffering through bureaucracy; enduring thirst and hunger; meticulous planning and calculation that, gone just a little bit wrong, might spell disaster. And we also could say that nonhuman animals are important for Reichardt's interests in interrelationship and environment. To understand how all of these interests are linked, we might consider the everyday details of the Hurricane Katrina disaster, one of *Wendy and Lucy*'s inspirations (Van Sant). One of the most notorious aspects to come to light later on was the fact that survivors were not allowed to bring their pets with them when evacuating, and that many rescue crews refused to save cats and dogs. A much-circulated Associated Press story centered on "Snowball," a little boy's dog that was confiscated by a police officer as the boy boarded a bus to the Superdome. According to AP reporter Mary Foster, the boy "cried until he vomited." Meanwhile, the police officer told another reporter "he didn't know what would happen to the dog"—the inverse of the fate of Lucy the dog, whose supposedly reckless owner Wendy leaves her only after knowing the dog will be well cared for. The "Snowball" story, the destruction of the New Orleans Aquarium, and the tagging of homes by the American Society for the Protection and Care of Animals with the same X-pattern as the human-rescue teams, all offer stark reminders of nonhuman animal lives devastated by Katrina. We might also note that the name "Snowball" was particularly resonant with the public considering the notion—which, as we argue, animates Reichardt's work—of the ever-accumulating troubles of those living on the economic and environmental fringe. Indeed, a film like *Wendy and Lucy* is about nothing if not the ways in which minor mistakes and misfortunes snowball into larger or, at least, longer, problems—leading, in fact, in Wendy's particular case, to the loss of one's beloved dog. As both noun (the dog) and verb, "Snowball" suggests that disaster happens through accretion; it does not befall one all at once as a spectacular, isolated moment.

Activists such as Karen Dawn opined after Katrina that "There is a class issue involved" with the restrictions on rescuing animals. She noted that "While Marriott hotels welcomed the pets of Katrina evacuees as 'part of the family,' people who had to rely on the Red Cross for shelter were forced to abandon that part of the family or attempt to ride out the storm. It cannot be denied that many poor people are dead as a result of 'no pets' policies." We would agree with Dawn's analysis, but we also would extend it in saying that the poignancy of these stories emerges not from the vulnerability of the nonhuman animals left behind, nor that of their owners and keepers, but from the fact that these vulnerable people *had been* caretakers; had been embedded in a network of care and reciprocation, the likes of which was extended to them only unevenly thereafter. That is to say, the poignancy arises both from the irony of those who care not being properly cared *for*, and from the fact that these people had responsibilities and interdependencies that were not recognized or validated. Put even more pointedly, during Hurricane Katrina, classism and racism took the form (not to mention other forms) of not seeing survivors as having culture or ecology, which includes, among other things, geographic roots and relations with other species. Semiparadoxically, then, the classist and racist dehumanization of Katrina victims was manifested in how their care for nonhuman species was utterly rejected.

Enough of an outcry was made over this pattern of events to prompt the passage of the Federal Pets Evacuation and Transportation Standards Act in 2006 and to start a higher-profile discussion on nonhuman animals as companions and members of human families. And although this law marks the start of an important conversation of how classism and racism against humans shapes how we approach relationships with nonhuman animals, it remains centered on the humans involved in states of emergency. Here, we wish to take nonhuman animals on their own terms as a way of understanding the more radical and antianthropocentric edge of Reichardt's cinema. To begin with, her films frequently consider nonhuman animals as survivors, suggesting the ways they can persist after their human companions' departure. For example, *River of Grass* features an overhead shot of dead people and a living dog; "Four outta five murder victims are pet owners," says a cop, explaining Cozy's father's habit of adopting crime scene pets. The film's consistently ironic stance allows viewers to, first, imagine that an animal could count as a survivor; and, second, through the official-sounding count, to have a moment of hyperbolic statistical comedy—the image of a world overrun by animals owned by those four out of five humans. *River of Grass* undercuts the seriousness of the "four outta five" statistic with an image of Jimmy attempting to wash blood off a hamster in the sink. Jimmy's insistence that the hamster enter some state of clean respectability is clearly played for laughs, perhaps questioning Jimmy's application of human states of rectitude, affect, and mourning across species boundaries.

Similarly, the recurring presence of Reichardt's dog Lucy in *Old Joy* and *Wendy and Lucy* reminds us that we cannot impose human understandings of attachment and loss onto animals. In both films, Lucy shows her capacity for getting along with anyone, regardless of her owners' claims to the contrary ("she gets separation anxiety"). For example, Lucy's frequent appearance alongside *Old Joy*'s Kurt, rather than her owner Mark, suggests the flexibility of the dog's attachments. And though the end of *Wendy and Lucy* perhaps seems sad to us in the way the end of *Old Joy* does—a friendship is ending because its participants will no longer spend time together—Lucy will likely, and quickly, forge a new relationship with the person bringing her food. Jon Raymond's prose makes this point even more explicit. When our protagonist encounters the crust punks in his source story, she is wary, but her dog guileless, allowing one of them to pet her. As Raymond describes it, "Verna watched Lucy closely for some spark of affection [toward Verna], but her dog was too engrossed in the [other] girl's attention to look up, too busy giving herself away. Lucy panted heavily, her eyes half closed" (209). Later, a bitter epiphany: "A dog could love anyone, [Verna] thought. A dog could be happy almost anywhere. They just needed food and water and affection. They were not picky about who delivered it. And by the same token, a dog could forget anyone, too. They were loyal, but only to whoever was around" (258).

Then, a Year takes the concept of nonhuman, and indifferent, survivors of an emergency furthest, using its experimental form to reveal a world that does not miss its humans, thereby challenging viewers for whom humans are the normal center of filmic and narrative interest. The film portrays a landscape clearly created in the aftermath of a human departure, whether these people have departed for more habitable climes, or disappeared through some violent crisis.[64] The obviously recorded nature of the human speech found in the film—the true-crime voiceover commentary—as well as its clearly nondiegetic relation to the film's images, gives it a black-box recorder quality. These are sounds from another time, a time before people abandoned the film's setting. That landscape seems to be a working-class Oregon suburb gone wild: The film's images include tracking shots of a neighborhood from a car window, zoom-ins on leaves and blossoms, a black-and-white pan of a cat stalking by, repeated images of leaves and a waterfall, and low-angle shots of birds on telephone wires. Though *Then, a Year* does capture remains of human life—zooming in on an unmade bed, an ashtray full of cigarette butts, and a kitchen timer with the ticker at zero—the image track perversely resists the kind of anthropocentric questions and comments posed by the soundtrack: "Not only, who done it, so to speak? But why they done it, so to speak?"; "The only thing that would prove worse than the mystery was the truth." There is no human voice from within the image world to answer back, or to tell us "the truth." We might then posit that the camera and the editing's refusal to make recognizable meaning is a sign of the way Reichardt's films give room to nonhuman others. The film presents artifacts that do not give up their secrets in response to a human viewer's gaze, and animal and plant beings that maintain their radical alterity in the face of viewers' desire to know. *Then, a Year* offers an account of life "in the after" that does not depend upon human lives or even perspectives.

The possibility of unequal reciprocal feeling on the part of nonhuman animals toward their human companions—not to mention the specter of a posthuman world overrun by cats, birds, hamsters, and various flora—may be a bit unsettling for the humans among us. But we want to suggest that a kind of ethics underline this radical unsentimentality. By emphasizing nonhuman animals' status as survivors, and suggesting the way they can persist after their human companions' departure, Reichardt gives weight to the importance of nonhuman life in its own right. To be clear, then, we do not wish to claim that Lucy, Snowball, or the hamster do not care about losing their owners—nor do we wish to claim that they *do* care. We can never truly know either way. Our point is that, even while Reichardt validates the affective bonds between humans and their animals—pointing out the way a cruel society is unwilling to recognize Wendy's attachment to a dog she cannot afford to feed, for example—she also challenges the human tendency to imagine animal lives only in relation to our own. In this way, Reichardt seems to engage with the ideas articulated by theorist Donna Haraway in her *Companion Species Manifesto*: "all ethical relating, within or between species, is knit from the silk-strong thread of ongoing alertness to otherness-in-relation. We are not one, and being depends on getting on together" (50).

Reichardt's comments about filming animals are particularly illuminating in this context. When we asked her in our interview about the recurrence of nonhuman figures in her films, Reichardt spoke about the enlivening effect the oxen had on the human performers in *Meek's Cutoff*: "The animals added a level of real danger, where the actors had to be so present in paying attention to what they're doing." She explained, further, that oxen in particular are unpredictable—which is why westerns have, somewhat inaccurately, preferred to show horses. In Reichardt's discussion of the kind of presence these animals require of their human costars, we see that her films encourage nonhierarchical and nonanthropomorphic interaction between human and nonhuman actors. The human actors have to deal with nonhuman animals on their own terms, which means neither taking them for granted nor making sentimental assumptions about them.

It may seem contradictory to claim that a filmmaker who cares about, say, a mother's grief, could be so pointedly agnostic about a dog's or hamster's grief. Reichardt's antianthropocentrism is a piece with the anti-individualist, antisentimental, and social-realist commitments that we have described throughout this book. In the same way that she explores the possibility of ethical relationships with those humans with whom we don't or can't identify, Reichardt reminds us that there are other beings in the world that may resist identification or understanding. The important thing is to *act ethically nonetheless*—whether or not we can comprehend or accurately grasp motivation or intent. After all, to one viewer or another, a Wendy or a Josh may be just as inscrutable as a hamster or a bird, if not more so. Finally, although Reichardt never collapses the two categories, her treatment of human and nonhuman survivors has similar effects: in focusing on the emergent moments of aftermath, Reichardt's films frame survival not as a state of exception but as an everyday matter.

Thus, although not a celebration of individual lives, we might say that Reichardt's cinema gives an account of the way *life carries on*—even despite increasingly inhospitable and austere conditions, and, therefore, with no guarantee of the life in question being a "good" one. It is an account that is simultaneously hopeful and devastating.

Notes

1. According to David Bordwell ("Measurement Theory"), the average contemporary film shot lasts four to six seconds.

2. For example, the *Oxford English Dictionary*'s fourth definition for *emerge* is "To rise into notice, come forth from obscurity; also, to issue *from* a state of subjection, suffering, embarrassment, etc."

3. See, for example, Perren, 144.

4. See also Stephen Holden's *New York Times* review, which declared that *River of Grass* "is wonderful at conveying a sense of suffocating ennui. Too wonderful, since the story is so sketchily told and the dialogue is so fragmentary that it doesn't quite cohere."

5. LeGros appeared in *Night Moves* and *Certain Women*; Oldham in *Old Joy* and *Wendy and Lucy*; Patton in *Wendy and Lucy* and *Meek's Cutoff*; and Williams in *Wendy and Lucy*, *Meek's Cutoff*, and *Certain Women*.

6. *Old Joy*, for instance was filmed around Portland and in the Mount Hood area visited by the protagonists. *Wendy and Lucy* was set in Wilsonville, part of the Portland metropolitan area, and filmed primarily in Portland. *Meek's Cutoff* was filmed in the desert areas of eastern Oregon, and *Night Moves* was filmed in southern Oregon. Although the real Wilsonville is more of a middle-class suburb, Reichardt renders it as the kind of declining working-class town that one might find in areas such as Washington County, Oregon.

Then, a Year was filmed in Portland and features transcripts of letters from the case of teacher Mary Kay LeTourneau and her student in suburban Washington state, and the bereaved mother at the center of *Travis* is a Portland-based antiwar activist, Lynn Bradach. See regional coverage of the latter at http://www.thestranger.com/seattle/mourning-in-america/Content?oid=23114.

As noted, Reichardt has moved from Oregon to Montana as of the recently released *Certain Women*. But one could still point to an Oregon connection, albeit distant: Maile Meloy, author of the source material, is the sister of the well-known Portland musician Colin Meloy (The Decemberists).

7. In addition to casting "authentic train-hopping gutter punks" (Van Sant interview) in *Wendy and Lucy*, for the sneering stock boy Andy she cast Portland-born John Robinson, perhaps best known for his role in Portland-born director Gus Van Sant's *Elephant* (2003), set in Portland. And Ayanna Berkshire, who plays the pound employee in *Wendy and Lucy*, would be familiar to the average viewer for her small role that same year in *Twilight* (directed by Catherine Hardwicke, 2008)—arguably the most famous Pacific Northwest film.

8. See A. O. Scott ("part of a recent wave of independent filmmakers who take up contemporary issues while referencing class-conscious, midcentury neorealists such as Vittorio De Sica and Roberto Rossellini") and Romney ("the varied strain of austere minimalist cinema that has thrived internationally over the past ten years" [43]).

9. His version of the story would appear as "Train Choir" in his collection *Livability*, alongside a republished "Old Joy." As Reichardt explained to one interviewer, "With 'Wendy and Lucy' we came up with the story line together and then Jon wrote the short and I started working on the script while he was still writing and then he started working on the script" (Perry); "Train Choir" thus appeared in print in *Livability* the same month (December 2008) that *Wendy and Lucy* opened in theaters.

10. See Geoff King's *Indiewood*, where he argues that "where departures from mainstream convention are found at the formal level, they tend to be in two main directions: either in making greater claims to verisimilitude/realism, or in the use of more complex, stylized, expressive, showy or self-conscious forms" (10).

11. See images at https://www.cinematerial.com/movies/river-of-grass-i110998/p/jpp6vw4r and http://www.impawards.com/1994/river_of_grass.html.

12. The only other film that comes close is *Wendy and Lucy*, in which a track of the protagonist's humming is laid over a scene of her walking aimlessly. The difference here is crucial: stripped of her modes of transportation and survival, Wendy's consciousness cannot break through to us in anything so articulate and humanizing as words.

13. Here, Reichardt departs from Jon Raymond's source stories, which more extensively sketch out protagonists' backgrounds.

14. Indeed, "Cozy" is the most unique protagonist name in Reichardt's œuvre, and one of the only unique names on the whole; a supporting character named Surprise appears in *Night Moves*, but she is presented semisatirically, as a hippie organic farmer who offers to read people's auras.

15. King explains that the "quirkiness" of indie characters, now a cliché in its own right, is inherently un-Marxist (250), a charge made much earlier by Georg Lukács in *The Historical Novel*, where he understood the grotesqueries of literary naturalism and modernism (as opposed to realism) as a reduction of historical processes into individualistic pathologies—or, to use King's term, "quirks." In this way, Lukács argues, certain kinds of realism fail as Marxist critique because in them all history is routed through the individual.

16. Something similar happens in the *River of Grass* scenes focused on African-American men.

17. Fessenden's career since has included significant work on independent horror features such as *Wendigo* (2001), suggesting his difference in sensibility from Reichardt.

18. Much further below, we discuss the problematic implications of this term.

19. When doing press for *Wendy and Lucy*, Reichardt challenged an interviewer to name any female filmmaker who "can insist on creative control and still raise 20 million." She then says, "Okay, forget about 20 million. Name a woman at the level of Gus Van Sant or Todd Haynes [both friends of Reichardt]. Give me a female example of that [level of independent success]" (Stewart).

20. IMDB estimates the production costs of *Old Joy* and *Wendy and Lucy* as $300,000 and $200,000, respectively.

21. We draw our definition from André Bazin's many essays on the movement and De Sica's exemplary body of work.

22. Throughout her career, Ashby's film remains an important influence on Reichardt. In an interview promoting *Wendy and Lucy*, for example, she calls *Shampoo* "an ideal political film" (Stewart).

23. Indeed, even if we understand Reichardt as working with genres other than the road movie—including the western (*Meek's Cutoff*) and the thriller (*Night Moves*)—we see that she invokes generic tropes only to disappoint them: Although the road movie, western, and thriller are typically characterized by motifs such as mobility, openness, and mastery, her films' plots and visuals push in the opposite direction, encountering literal and figurative immobility (geographic, social, and economic) and precarity.

24. We arrived at this insight thanks to the 2016 Modern Language Association panel "Security, the Public, and the Twenty-First-Century United States Novel," featuring Allison Carruth, Samuel Cohen, and Gordon Hutner, with comments from Alison Shonkwiler.

25. Besides eschewing backstories and conclusive endings, Reichardt's *Meek's Cutoff* restricts viewers' (and, of course, characters') perspectives, as we discuss later.

26. Reichardt's source text, Raymond's "Train Choir," creates similar dramatic irony by focalizing the narrative through the protagonist, Vera: "For a moment, under the spilling stars, almost exactly halfway from Muncie, Indiana, to easy money in the Alaskan fisheries, she allowed herself a brief *intuition* of better times to come. In four more days *they would be in Alaska*" (207, our emphasis). Later, she imagines, "In Ketchikan [Alaska] she would be able to start drawing from her first paycheck immediately, and from then on she would be all right" (212). For any reader who has had to endure lean times until the first paycheck—or who has experienced precarious life, more generally—Vera's "plan" seems dubious, to say the least. And, of course, they never do make it to Alaska.

27. To be clear, Reichardt never encourages us to blame *any* individuals in her films; not the downtrodden, like Wendy, or, on the other hand, authority figures like the cops or even the self-righteous stock boy—who, in a different film, would be the bad guy. In Reichardt's films, we find people forced to act out positions even when they mean nothing personal by it. We might recall here Bazin's comments about neorealist master De Sica's films: "in *Miracolo a Milano* . . . none of the bad people, even the proud or treacherous ones, are antipathetic. . . . [N]one of the principal characters in *Ladri di Biciclette* is unsympathetic. Not even the thief" (69). Or, as Raymond puts it in the source material story "Train Choir," after the security guard has told our protagonist to move her car, she "sensed immediately he had no real problem with her, just a job to do" (213).

28. One could argue that, in a perverse way, the stock boy and manager's detention and eventual prosecution of Wendy for shoplifting is a gesture of inclusion. Although she protests that, since she's not from around there, she can't be made an example of, the two insist that she be detained on principle. By the logic of this exchange, Wendy is being held to the same rules as any member of the community would.

29. Such an understanding is a distinct misconstrual, many of us would say, as is shown by how Walmart's unjust employment policies have kept many of their workers in relative poverty while members of its founding family regularly place among the top ten richest people in the world. For information on the Walton family's wealth, see http://www.forbes.com/forbes-400/top20/#6286b1cbd8d5. Walmart's notorious employment policies were most famously brought to light by Barbara Ehrenreich in her 2001 work of undercover journalism, *Nickel and Dimed: On (Not) Getting By in America*. As many readers likely know, the thesis of Ehrenreich's book was that, even at full-time or near-full-time employment at a place such as Walmart, she could not earning a living wage and in fact had to live out of her car, like Reichardt's Wendy.

30. Raymond's story makes its protagonist hyperaware of this fact, sometimes even making her jealous of her own dog: Lucy "had no trouble making friends on the road" ("Train Choir," 209), Verna complains bitterly. Of course, the reason is that she demands relatively little, because she can't be blamed for her bad circumstances, and because her demands can be construed as instinctive—unlike her owner's needs.

31. Dana Stevens deems it such in her essay on the film in *Slate*.

32. As Jim Kitses observes, the "dialectical scheme" ordering the western plot—that is, of the West as either garden or desert, either refuge from the corrupt East or den of savagery in need of civilizing—"positions the Western hero between the nomadic and the settled, the savage and the cultured, the masculine and feminine." He argues that "This interplay of ideas accounts for the charged racial and sexual dynamics of the genre, wherein the Indian and the woman can be constructed principally as archetypal agents that define the hero's direction" (13).

33. This dynamic may explain why, despite their relatively short lengths (*Old Joy* runs 76 minutes and *Wendy and Lucy* runs 80, for example), Reichardt's films feel quite long.

34. Other contemporary filmmakers associated with slow cinema are Lisandro Alonso (Argentina), Semih Kaplanoğlu (Turkey), and Apichatpong Weerasethakul (Thailand). It should be noted, however, that criticism and scholarship on slow cinema often invokes older figures such as Chantal Akerman (Belgium), Theo Angelopoulos (Greece), and Béla Tarr (Hungary).

35. Strangely, Jaffe's extensive book does not mention Kelly Reichardt, even in passing.

36. Slow cinema has occasioned much debate among professional film critics and film bloggers (and, to a much lesser degree, film scholars), down to the very term itself. Film blogger Harry Tuttle of *Unspoken Cinema* has suggested the term "contemporary contemplative cinema," apparently because "slow" so often functions as a negative criticism of a film. And, in a controversial 2010 piece for the British Film Institute's magazine *Sight and Sound*, editor Nick James wrote, "The bargain the newer variety of slow films seem to impose on the viewer is simple: it's up to you to draw on your stoic patience and the fascination in your gaze, in case you miss a masterpiece. Watching a film like the Berlin Golden Bear-winner *Honey* [AKA *Bal*, dir. Semih Kaplanoğlu, 2010] . . . you feel an implicit threat: admit you're bored and you're a philistine" (5). This is a strange suggestion: that, in watching slow cinema, one might be exposed as "unclassy," part of the masses—when, in fact, the very act of watching slow cinema in the first place usually marks one as part of a unique intellectual or cultural (if not economic) class. (And, moreover, it's those *onscreen* in slow cinema that are, usually, part of the masses.) Without speculating too much here on viewership, we suspect that Reichardt's cinema assumes viewers that are part of an elite class; it then asks them whether they can feel sympathy for the more down-and-out characters they see onscreen. At the same time, it seems that Kois and others' critiques of slow cinema as boring are predicated on a particular fear: that, in failing to "stay classy" and appreciate these films, viewers might fall out of the upper class—a taste-based parallel to what's happening onscreen at the level of economics, with Reichardt's downwardly mobile protagonists.

37. After giving his sister-in-law a tour of his rural farm, for instance, protagonist Boonmee confesses that he believes his terminal illness is "a result of my karma. I've killed too many Communists. And I've killed a lot of bugs on my farm." (These characters are devoutly Buddhist, which is why reincarnation and ghosts, which are of course phenomena of time, are so prominent in the film.) And while Boonmee appears to be an otherwise benevolent farm owner and boss, many of the film's discussions center on his decision to employ undocumented immigrants from bordering Laos. These discussions resonate ironically with lead actor Thanapat Saisaymar's *real life* status not as a farm owner or even professional actor but as a farmhand, himself working on the border of Thailand and Laos.

38. A transnational perspective, as well as a cross-class perspective, is important here. For example, in response to film scholar Steven Shaviro's blog critique of recent slow cinema films, one commenter pointed out that "the films of [Turkish directors such as Semih Kaplanoğlu] do not appear specifically slow to the audience in a country like Turkey that never had a 'fast' cinema . . . and that 'yet another woodland path' in *Bal* [*Honey*] that [Nick James] speaks of is in fact a part of the country (the Blacksea coast) rarely captured or dealt with in Turkish cinema (hence the silence of its inhabitants; they are invisible, voiceless, in contrast with the all too vibrant and sonorous quality of their environment)." See http://www.shaviro.com/Blog/?p=891.

39. See also Gorfinkel's 2012 essay in *Discourse*, "Weariness, Waiting: Enduration and Art Cinema's Tired Bodies," which also discusses Reichardt.

40. Indeed, Schoonover's sense of the economic and political implications of slowness, boredom, activity, and stasis builds on a long philosophical tradition that has its roots in Kierkegaard's industrial revolution musings; the latter observes that in the attempt to not be idle, man responds with "an indefatigable activity that shuts a person out of the world of spirit and places him in a class with the animals, which instinctively must always be in motion. There are people who have an extraordinary talent for transforming everything into a business operation, whose whole life is a business operation, who fall in love and are married, hear a joke, and admire a work of art with the same businesslike zeal with which they work at the office" (54). Even in nineteenth-century Europe, then, idleness is that which must be disavowed.

41. Whereas Nixon focuses primarily on creeping environmental degradation and related social injustices in the contemporary Global South, we argue that the specifically U.S. postindustrial downward mobility depicted in Reichardt's films also constitutes an instance of slow violence.

42. Widescreen formats, used as early as 1897 but developed and popularized most extensively in the 1950s, have greatly contributed to what we tend to think of as the "classic" look of a western.

43. For example, consider the contrast of other works focused on boredom, from Bret Easton Ellis's novels *Less Than Zero* (1985) and *The Rules of Attraction* (1987), in which disaffected young people experiment with drugs and sex, to Tamar van den Dop's film *Supernova* (2014), in which a restless Dutch teenager longs for a car to crash into her rural roadside house.

44. We might consider here Martin Esslin's claim that "'it is in the act of waiting that we experience the flow of *time* in its purest, most evident form. If we are active, we tend to forget the passage of time, we *pass* the time, but if we are merely passively waiting, we are confronted with the action of time itself'" (as quoted in Jaffe, 11–12, emphasis original).

45. Philosopher Lars Svendson captures this experience of time when he observes, "Boredom . . . arises when we cannot do what we want to do, or have to do something we do not want to do. *But what about when we have no idea*

about what we want to do, when we have lost the capacity to get our bearings in life?" (19, our emphasis). Though Svendson describes this boredom as one that afflicts all citizens of our age, Reichardt demonstrates the ways in which such boredom is particular to the working-class and down-and-out characters who populate her landscapes. Neorealism understood this connection as well; when De Sica's Umberto D. finds himself evicted by his landlady, he responds by checking in to the state hospital, where his real, material need for shelter drives him to waste time for a week.

46. *Night Moves* is, of course, another temporal title—and an ironic one at that, for the characters' decision to bomb a dam greatly circumscribes their freedom and mobility, even their ability to communicate freely, thereafter.

47. As Jaffe notes, "the sparse narratives [of slow movies] usually adhere to the present moment, to what D. N. Rodowick calls 'chronological time', 'time experienced as succession in the present'"—as opposed to "nonlinear, more complex time, wherein aspects of the real and the imaginary, and of past, present and future"—and, we might add, simultaneity, or parallel time—"commingle" (5). We take issue, of course, with the implication that the linear time of a filmmaker like Reichardt is not complex, or that it fails to show past, present, and future commingling.

Certain Women does feature multiple plots, as we have noted. None is a subplot of another, however, and each story is presented sequentially and given a significant amount of time. (See the discussion of *Certain Women* in "Processing Emergency.")

48. Reichardt frequently includes sounds of breathing. We argue that this indexes her interest in labor and pace more generally. The time of Reichardt's films is the time of living, laboring bodies, whether human or nonhuman.

49. David Thomas Sumner and Lisa Weidman have argued that the term "ecoterrorism" has become an inappropriate euphemism for radical environmental activism. On "ecoterrorism" in Oregon, see, for example, the FBI's Operation Backfire (https://www.fbi.gov/news/stories/2008/november/backfire_11908) or the case of Eric McDonald (http://www.sacbee.com/news/local/article7251650.html). On the state bills, see http://www.mintpressnews.com/so-called-eco-terrorism-law-in-oregon-would-add-special-penalties-to-environmental-activism/81607/.

50. See Seymour, *Strange Natures* (8) for a discussion of how the BP Deepwater Horizon disaster highlighted corporate disregard for longevity.

51. In 2014, the U.S.-based Pacific Institute, a nonprofit research institution, found that violent confrontations over water had increased fourfold during the last decade. As their president Peter Gleick told *The Guardian*, "I think the risk of conflicts over water is growing—not shrinking—because of increased competition . . . and, ultimately, because of the impacts of climate change" (Goldenburg). A U.S. intelligence report released the year before *Night Moves* had similar findings. See http://www.dni.gov/files/documents/Special%20Report_ICA%20Global%20Water%20Security.pdf.

52. Though Reichardt's *Night Moves* shares little in plot with Penn's neo-noir, the film does focus on a detective (Gene Hackman) tracking down a wealthy young runaway named Delly (Melanie Griffith) who, her mother thinks, has gone off to hang out with "freaks." There may be a parallel here between Delly and Dena, both young, wealthy runaways who have fallen in with countercultural elements. Alongside *Shampoo*, Penn's film is yet another Reichardt intertext that captures the end of the idealistic 1960s and the beginning of an era in which the counterculture has been corrupted or reduced to little more than sex and drugs.

53. Further, Burchfield and Reichardt have a similarity of milieu; the painter documented U.S. industry in the early twentieth century, already suggesting the tension between natural plentitude and commercial waste in paintings of steel towns and shanties alongside railroad tracks. At the same time that Burchfield captured a sense of waste, he also seemed to celebrate industry, as in his series of Buffalo, New York, paintings such as *Railroad in Spring* (1933) and *Grain Elevators* (1931–38). These ambiguous paintings, created in the first half of the twentieth century, capture the types of industry that Reichardt shows to have declined by the century's close. For our discussion of Burchfield, we draw from pp. 143 and 153 in John I. H. Baur's *The Inlander: The Life and Work of Charles Burchfield, 1893–1967*.

54. Like the protagonist of *River of Grass*, which was released five years later, Holloway was an unremarkable woman leading a stifled domestic existence whose foray into criminality backfired pathetically, making her a figure of ridicule. Holloway became the subject of the 1993 HBO film, *The Positively True Adventures of the Alleged Texas Cheerleader-Murdering Mom*, which shares with *River of Grass* a comedic approach to criminality, as well as a regionalist sensibility.

55. First proposed by biologist Eugene Stoermer and popularized by chemist Paul Crutzen, the term *Anthropocene* represents the idea that we are currently in a distinct epoch, one in which humans have emerged as a geological force in their own right. The term has prompted various periodizations—with scholars citing start dates ranging from eight thousand years ago, to the Industrial Revolution, to 1945—and much controversy over its political implications. See, for instance, the May 2015 "Race and the Anthropocene" symposium at the University of Oregon.

56. *Night Moves* was released two months after Edward Snowden's famous National Security Administration whistle-blowing in 2013.

For more on public apathy toward the NSA surveillance, see http://www.washingtonpost.com/politics/most-americans-support-nsa-tracking-phone-records-prioritize-investigations-over-privacy/2013/06/10/51e721d6-d204–11e2–9f1a-1a7cdee20287_story.html. Public support for the program has diminished over time, however. See, for example, http://www.usatoday.com/story/news/politics/2014/01/20/poll-nsa-surveillance/4638551/.

57. "emerge, v." *OED Online*. Oxford University Press, June 2016. Web. 10 June 2016.

58. See full lyrics at http://www.metrolyrics.com/ode-to-billie-joe-lyrics-bobbie-gentry.html.

59. It is interesting that, although the narrator seems to be heterodiegetic, he has a pronounced Southern accent like the characters in the film.

60. See, for example, the story of Rutgers University student Tyler Clementi, who jumped off the George Washington Bridge into the Hudson River in 2010 after being tormented by his roommate.

61. See link to lyrics in note 58. The song's narrator never offers her own name, but the character Bobbie Lee Hartley, who appears in subsequent adaptations, is clearly her equivalent. "Bobbie Lee Hartley," of course, seems to play off of Bobbie Gentry's name; in addition to their shared first names, Gentry's middle name also is Lee.

62. Although Kurt is a domestic scavenger, the latter item in particular might remind us of the real fate of contemporary U.S. waste—with up to 80 percent of our outdated electronics being exported to less developed countries (Greenpeace). In recent times, as figures ranging from postcolonial scholar Sarah Harrison to the activist group Greenpeace have suggested, gleaning's relationship to aftermath has taken an industrial and globalized turn as developed cities and countries export their waste to impoverished spaces. See Harrison's *Waste Matters: Urban Margins in Contemporary Literature*.

63. See http://www.brooklynrail.org/2014/07/criticspage/after-anthropocinema and Selmin Kara's essay "Anthropocinema: Cinema in the Age of Mass Extinctions," in Julia Leyda and Shane Denson's *Post-Cinema: Theorizing 21st Century Film*.

64. Elsewhere, Seymour has argued that this kind of *World without Us* (Alan Weisman) rhetoric can have problematic implications. (See Seymour, "Down with People: Queer Tendencies and Troubling Racial Politics in Antinatalist Discourse," in Estok, Gaard, and Oppermann's *International Perspectives in Feminist Ecocriticism*.) For example, some texts in this vein seem to take glee in the idea of humans being erased from the face of the earth—thus, among other things, glossing over a long history of unequal eradication, especially of people of color, through genocide, colonization, and other means. We propose here, though, that Reichardt's antianthropocentrism is not only subtle but inherently ethical in its thrust.

An Interview with Kelly Reichardt

We interviewed Kelly Reichardt at home in Queens, New York, on March 27, 2013. Pinned to Reichardt's office bulletin board was a photograph of a vintage car and an ad for Monte Hellman's 1971 road movie, *Two-Lane Blacktop*. Lucy the dog, of *Old Joy* and *Wendy and Lucy* fame, was in attendance.

Q: From what we've read, it seems that there are some autobiographical elements in your films, especially *River of Grass*. To what degree do you think of your films as autobiographical?

A: Funny, I was reading something this morning and I thought, "Ah, I'm so sick of the personal story." It's like what Fran Lebowitz writes: "Everyone *doesn't* need to tell their story." In *River of Grass* there are autobiographical elements: I shot in the area I grew up in, and my father's a crime-scene detective down there. But that's all. I didn't abandon any children or anything like that! To me, it was more of a landscape film, and playing on the road movie genre. But since then, I don't think

I've done anything that's felt at all autobiographical. Although, in *Wendy and Lucy*, it's my dog! And, well, I guess in *Old Joy* there were elements of Kurt [that ring true for me]: at the time, I had been couch-hopping for five years in New York and was really displaced for too long. And it was really wearing on relationships. So, stuff sneaks in, but it's certainly not my intention. Working with [screenwriter] Jon Raymond has kept things from being really autobiographical, in a way that's good, I think, and interesting. Because it's just nice to step into a different world and investigate something and figure something out. In these last movies, the first seed of ideas have been Jon's, because I'm usually editing the last film and then he asks, "What about this?" The Northwest is not something I grew up with.

Q: People talk about your last three movies as being the "Oregon trilogy"—how did you end up making several movies in a row centered on the Northwest?

A: After Todd Haynes [the filmmaker; Reichardt's close friend and sometime producer] made *Safe*, another friend and I drove him from the Seattle Film Festival down to Portland and I was there for a day. It was a rainy, classic Portland day. And such a different landscape from where I had been living in New York, and certainly different than Miami. I'd traveled around a lot, but I hadn't been in the great Northwest. I was just there for that day, but when Todd moved out there in 1998 I started going out there to visit him. I made a short film out there, and I met Jon Raymond—just briefly, but Todd gave me his novel *The Half Life*. So I read it and then asked Jon if he had any short stories. And then I ended up meeting my producer Neil Kopp out there, who I made *Old Joy* with [based on a Raymond short story of the same name], and a community of people that we've been making films with. But Jon is from Oregon and very settled there, and that's what he really writes about. Now I've ended up having quite a lot of my life spent out there; I spend probably half the year out there now. I've been in New York for a long time, so I don't want to make a film here. But I don't know; we may have worn Oregon out at this point!

Q: How does being a "working filmmaker" influence the kind of films you make? So, you're teaching . . .

A: Oh, I'm so glad you didn't say "woman filmmaker"!

Q: [Laughter.] Oh, no. We decided not to ask that question!

A: I appreciate that! I really appreciate it. So, the question is, a "working filmmaker" . . . ?

Q: Yes, a teacher also . . .

A: Oh, I see. Because I was going to say, "I also have another job!" Well, one thing is that the films have all been very small and I've really had complete freedom in making them. I have final cut, I don't have to adjust the script, and people are either in or they're out. We take small amounts of money to make these films, in exchange for the artistic freedom I have. But you know, you come back with a broken-down car, you don't come back with money to live off of. So teaching is a good balance for that. Bard in particular, for me, has been a great experience. I sort of think of teaching as being at Bard. I work with Peggy Ahwesh and Peter Hutton and Jackie Goss, who are all filmmakers that I really admire, and who make films so completely differently than I do. So Young Kim's teaching there now . . . and it's just such a small, intimate place. I just showed my colleagues a very rough cut of *Night Moves*—and, you know, you put six experimental filmmakers in a room, and you show them your narrative, you get really wacky notes! [Laughter.] I think it helps my teaching to be making something, and I think it helps my making to be in conversation about film all the time, and just exploring stuff, deconstructing forms, and being able to do that in an environment where there are these people working outside of a traditional form. Bard has been a really great match for me and is mostly what keeps me on the East Coast at this point.

Q: In interviews, you've mentioned a wide range of influences, from *Shampoo* to neorealism. What makes a film influential for you?

A: You know, that's another thing with teaching: you show a variety of things. But it's harder to say as you get older where your influences are coming from. Everyone talks about Robert Bresson, because Bresson has such clean lines, and it all looks so . . . simplistic in a way. It maybe feels achievable. I don't know what it is, what the magic is with Bresson; you break down all the elements and it doesn't look like those films should be as hard to achieve as they are. To me, they're just such perfect films. Oh God, I really hate the question about influence because it's so [time-dependent]. You could say, "I'm just going to dive into François Ozon for a while, and that would be what your head is about for a while. I use things that are easy to teach with, because the lines are clean, like Nicholas Ray and Douglas Sirk. And I use Todd Haynes's films a lot in my class, and they don't stop giving. I mean, I read those scripts, and I watched cuts of them, and I would sometimes be there, watching them be filmed, and I can teach them in a class for a really long time, and they still keep revealing things to me. I don't see as many films as I used to. I was doing my taxes recently, and I remember I used to have a whole pile of film stubs, and now it's just like a deck of cards. It's because I've been editing and making films—so that time of completely saturating yourself with going to the movies is not the period of time I'm in anymore. Which is sad, but that's how it goes. I just end up watching a lot of films that I'm teaching with.

Q: Well, it's a good motivational excuse. If you put something on a syllabus, then it's like, "Well, I guess I *have* to watch this, or read this!"

A: Oh, yeah. I direct my classes around what I need for filmmaking. . . . "westerns, we'll be doing westerns!"

Q: We wanted to ask you about so-called "slow cinema"—and not just your reaction to the designation itself, but how it feels being lumped in with other work with which you may or may not see yourself as affined.

A: I get lumped in with this "neorealism" a lot, often with a lot of films that feel more "filmsy" or experiential to me. I feel like my films are different, more structured. But it's all treated the same. And maybe it is! Maybe it is all realism. It's not really my job to decide! But I never feel that connected with supposed film movements. I try not to follow the dialogue around and try to be as sparse as possible and rely on the filmmaking as much as possible. I don't really have a bird's-eye view of it; you get so inside your own thing.

Sometimes I think films get paired together based on budget. Just the idea of independent cinema seems completely geared toward budget at this point, more than anything else. I mean, there are lots of low-budget films that are explicitly focused on the winners and the haves. And I always thought of experimental film as being about people who are sort of on the edges; not the people that would usually, you know . . .

Q: . . . get a story told about them.

A: Yes. Can you ask the question again?

Q: What do you think of being grouped under "slow cinema"?

A: Ah, slow cinema! Well, you know, there was that whole argument in the *New York Times*, which my films kept getting roped into. I forget who started it . . .

Q: Dan Kois; the article that compares watching slow cinema films to eating your vegetables. . . .

A: Yeah, "cultural vegetables." I don't think that everyone should have to eat their cultural vegetables; I just don't necessarily think you should write for the *Times* if you don't want to eat your cultural vegetables! I'm not out to make films that are *slow*, really. It's just that, when I go to the movies and I sit through the previews, I literally feel assaulted. And so maybe it's just people's metabolisms or something. I mean, okay, some of [my] films are about duration, have duration built into them. *Meek's* is about the labor it takes to walk across the country and the chores involved. So I understand that a slower pace is necessary for that film. But because it's so necessary to the story I don't think of it as being slow; I think of it as being the appropriate time for that story. And all the films are really about small moments and small decisions. You know, *Night Moves* is my "*action film*"—it's a thriller, with a small *t*. But ultimately it still breaks down to labor and chores: the things you have to do to do when you're doing what these kids are up to, this direct activism. But I really don't consider the films to be that slow. I mean, I work with Peter Hutton, and you sit on his couch and you watch a landscape film for three hours, and you've seen five shots. I like it! [Laughter.] But *my* films are not *slow*! I get told they're slow a lot, but . . . they're really short, first of all. What's everyone's problem?! Don't freak out at *me*! [Laughter.] *Night Moves* is not slow, though I showed a cut to someone yesterday and I said, "Oh my God, is the pacing just *too fast*??" And he said, "NOOOOOO." [Laughter.]

Q: We've read a couple interviews where you mention *Wendy and Lucy* having a Hurricane Katrina connection, and of course *Travis* is about the Iraq-Afghanistan war. And you were just talking about these small, everyday moments. So are you thinking of yourself as telling big stories through small moments, or . . .

A: No. Those events are all fine and good for early conversations, but those are really not what Jon and I talk about. We think about our characters and what they're going through. It's just that in interviews, you get a microphone in your hand, you can't help but talk about bigger things! Jon and Todd [Haynes] and I sit around and talk about politics all the time, because that's what we're interested in. But when I'm thinking about the movie, I certainly don't have those conversations with my actors, or my production designer, or my cinematographer. I think those conversations are there in the seeds of the screenplay at the very beginning, maybe, but not even. It's just what's in the air more. So I don't think we're making films about those events, though I think there are things about the films that are representative about the moment in America from a certain point of view.

Q: Your films, if we see them as westerns or road movies, seem like quintessential American cinema. But I wonder to what degree you think about yourself as working in that vein versus in a global sense—especially because your name's been linked to so many filmmakers from outside the United States.

A: I show cuts to people to get feedback, and I do look for people that are familiar with European cinema, because I think that we're not going to get hung up on conversations about pacing or certain approaches—things that are just easy for them to accept. With *Meek's* I had that Robert Adams book [on the American West] on me and his photographs were heavy in my mind. And when we were writing *Night Moves*, Jon Raymond turned me on to Charles Burchfield, and there just so happened to be this retrospective of him, and I got to see his paintings. And those colors, and the feelings of how he deals with nature, became very big in my mind. Those really "American" artists—Joel Sternfeld, Stephen Shore—that sort of American photography and American landscape, I feel really attached to. And I'd like to think I could go somewhere other than the U.S. and make a film, but I wouldn't really know how to step into that somewhere else. I'm drawn to images of American cinema and genres, American genres—but I am also really obviously drawn to, you know, Fassbinder. He's maybe the first filmmaker who blew my mind as a twenty-year-old, like, "Wow!"

Q: So we've been watching some of your short films—I hope that's okay! [Laughter.]

A. For me, those shorts are just about learning how to edit and things like that. I made such a strong attempt with *Then a Year* and *Travis* of trying to move away from narrative and step into this more avant-garde approach. And it's so unnatural for me. I just feel so ill suited to it. To me, a short film dealing with a short period of time seems so much harder than having time to let something play out. You know, you teach, and you see students all the time trying to do big things in a short amount of time. That doesn't work all that well! [Laughter.] I was coming to this point of not wanting to spend my life trying to raise money to make a big film, so I thought, "Well, maybe I can deal with the short format better if I just got away from story." I love experimental filmmaking, I love watching it, I'm drawn to it. But I don't have an affinity for it. Story just keeps trying to attach itself, and I spend so much time trying to unattach myself. When I would show these short films at festivals or whatever—with *Ode,* I think—I think it was Ken Jacobs—booed me. And that is a narrative film, but *Ode* was just such a beautiful filmmaking experience. Working with a crew of two people after trying to raise money for a really long time for a bigger film, just to go and hold your camera and hear the motor of your Super-8 camera in your hand, it was all just very fun and empowering and felt very "They can't keep us down!" I did it with my friend Susan Stover and it was just *fun*. I have an attachment to *Ode* from that experience, and I think the kids in it are really good. But the other short films are just me trying to figure out how in the world I'm going to make films. They feel like a forced fit to me, at least *Then a Year* is just so overedited. I mean, I think the editing is very bad in it! But anyway, I finally sat at the machine with myself and learned to edit.

Q: What do you think of the tenor of your work—or what are you aiming for? We ask in part because we both watched *River of Grass* after we'd seen your more recent films, and we were surprised that it was you! [Laughter.]

A: I know. [Laughter.]

Q: It has these almost slapstick moments; these overtly ironic, humorous comedic moments, and we just thought that was an interesting shift. Or maybe you don't perceive it as a shift.

A: It's funny because I remember at the time that everyone thought *River of Grass* lost its humor in the making of it, compared to the script, but some stuff survives. You know, I was trying to get on a show once and my agent said, "Oh they won't hire you, they want people with a sense of humor!" In *my world*, I'm *very funny*! [Laughter.] Jon and I have been talking about doing something lighter. You know, the '90s was such an optimistic time! Then all the themes got so heavy. I don't know what happened! Well, I know what happened. We moved into the Bush era, and it got fucking depressing! [Laughter.] Yeah, I don't know. . . . And

Jon Raymond sucked all of the humor—write this down, make sure you get this! He'll really appreciate it. Yeah, I don't know what happened. We got gloomier in our filmmaking.

Q: We wanted to ask you about the other people you've worked with. You've worked with both nonprofessional actors and professional actors, so what informs your decision about who you're going to cast?

A: [*Whispers.*] That's a political question. . . . It's funny; at first, you're kind of working with your friends because you don't have access to actors. And then you don't have access to money if you aren't casting actors. People say, "you're working with so many non-actors," but not really. People that are less famous, certainly. And then there's Michelle. Michelle had seen *Old Joy* and worked with Todd and was up for it, and I was like, "Oh, wow, *that's* great, what will *that* be like?" Working with someone technically experienced was a different experience, and a good one. Working with really experienced actors who give you a variety of things, you have a lot to work with in the editing process. If you're working with a nonprofessional actor, you're more saying, "I want you to be you onscreen!" Then, that is what you have. You're not making a bunch of choices along the way.

You never really know what the working relationship's going to be till you're on set. I have a short amount of time to have my actors, so usually we're rehearsing while we're shooting. It's a crapshoot; you don't know if people are gonna get there and be really into it and really down for it, or, you know, into it in theory and then the reality of how hard our fucking shoots can be sets in. And one could start to wonder if you could be doing other things—what you've gotten yourself into! And that can be really hard. What's good is if people have seen the films, and they know what they're in for. If, you come to a movie like *Meek's*, for example, and you have an idea of a traditional western in your mind, and you even have the majority of the dialogue, it would be your presumption that you're going to shoot a master shot, and then you're going to do it again, and then, eventually, after many takes, you're going to get your closeup, and you're going to work on that for a while. And when it's one take, and it's your big scene, and your back's to the camera, and you can't really hear your voice, your dialogue, there's no microphone near, you might start to get depressed! That you hauled your ass out in the 100-degree desert on a low-budget really hard film. [Laughter.] For anybody. I mean, actors have to be so trusting. They really have to totally turn themselves over to something. And not every actor wants to do that. And I wanna find the ones that do! [Laughter.] Cause I want things to be *my* way if they have to be somebody's way! [Laughter.] It's weird, you know, if you open the door on actors being able to bring their own ideas, it's a slippery slope, because that means everyone wants to do it. Some people are better at it than other people. And mostly I want people to stick with the script. I don't mind working on the script before we start shooting, but when you start changing dialogue when we're shooting, I'm not into that. There's room for as much small rehearsal time as we have in preproduction, and I'm into looking at things from whatever angle. But people always ask if we're doing a lot of improvising. And we're not.

Q: Well, this [indicating Lucy] is an actor who may or may not improvise: we know that your dog is one of your collaborators—

A: She's retired.

Q: She's retired?

A: Yeah.

Q: Well, we're really interested in the presence of animals throughout your movies. They're often onscreen, and they get a lot of space. So what are these animals doing in your films?

A: Will [Oldham] always said about Lucy in *Old Joy* that you have to respond to her, so you can stop thinking about what you're doing—because there's something else going on around you. You know, there's a dog shoving a stick at you, and you have to respond. He was saying how it made it easier to just sort of "be in the moment" of whatever he was doing. And I think that was probably true for Michelle [Williams, on *Wendy and Lucy*]. She had to respond to Lucy all the time also—and that's what she wants to do as an actor, is have something to respond to. So animals give you that. In *Meek's* it was certainly true! We were dealing with oxen instead of horses. I *knew* there were reasons people don't make westerns with oxen—though that's what it should be, historically speaking.

Q: We don't know about this. Are there terrible rumors about oxen?

A: Well, they're bulls, and they're not trained! You know, they're fine until they aren't. And they don't back up; they only walk in one direction. Once they get going, it's hard to stop. And they really just respond to voice things, like a dog, almost. Which was really interesting on *Meek* because when they were in trouble with the oxen, they would send in this woman who was my size; she was like, five-foot-nothing. And even in the river crossing, she would hop on their backs. There were a couple times when the oxen broke free, and you have a bull running through your set, and everyone holds their breath.

One time, just before a take, one of the bulls just started going for Michelle, and she just gave it the yell. 'Cause they had come out early. We had this "pioneer camp" where they had to learn to build fire, figure out everything that was going to go in their wagon, and learn how to deal with the bulls. And she just gave this stern call to the bull. And she stopped it in its tracks. And the wranglers who were off screen weren't able to stop him. Also, Shirley Henderson was really good. The oxen responded more to the women than the men. I don't know why, exactly, but it was pretty across-the-board that way; all the women were better drivers than the men. I mean, I have some footage of Paul Dano almost getting a horn in the gut. That no one got killed on that movie is amazing. People got killed because their dresses got caught under the wheels—I mean, in life, not on the movie set!

But it was the same for us; they were in the same outfits. For the women, they have blinders on—they can't see with those bonnets, they have no peripheral vision. And you're walking a bull that can charge at any second. Anything like that could happen. You know, we're using the wagons from the period, we're using oxen, we're aware the pioneers got lost where we were shooting. It's rattlesnake country. And it really was; it was rattlesnake season. The animals added a level of real danger, where the actors had to be so present in paying attention to what they're doing. And then we had a donkey and a mule. And the mule was a pain in the ass. The donkey, everyone really fell in love with. It was Shirley Henderson's donkey, and you couldn't walk by the donkey and not be like, "Ooohhh, the donkey, arrwwww!" I think animals keep everybody having to respond to something other than what's on the page, or in your mind.

Q: Having watched your films several times in a row, we've noticed this pattern of the hippy-type character who makes these big mystical pronouncements. There's the Kurt character from *Old Joy*, but also Icky from *Wendy and Lucy*, and then Meek from *Meek's Cutoff* . . .

A: There's a guy who shows up in *Night Moves*, too, and it's just like, "Ah, there you are, we've been waiting!" He just comes out of the woods, like, "Everybody, I'm the hippy character that all your movies have!" [Laughter.] You know, yeah. True. I think it's a northwestern thing. I would say that's very Jon Raymond. You can't spend time out there and not run across the mystical hippy people. On *Old Joy* the theme was sort of "Where are the mystical people supposed to go? The people who don't want to live the good Christian life, where are they supposed to be?" And then Icky . . . there's an Icky in life. Jon writes very close to people that are actually living and exist and sometimes it's gotten me into trouble. For *Night Moves*, we went and scouted a farm, and there was a guy in the script that Jon had written—and I know everything he writes is based on someone, but you never know how close it is. In this case, the name hadn't been changed, and it was the total guy! And it wasn't the greatest portrayal of the guy. I sent my scout to the guy's place, and my scout is innocently telling him about the character—describing him *to him*. And the guy has the same name. Wow, it was horrible. It was just so horrible. I remember calling Jon so mad and he was just mellow: "I almost feel responsible. . . ." Almost! What are you talking about? You could get us killed. [Laughter.] I don't know how Jon thinks he's going to get away with these things. I think he just knows that he won't be in the firestorm when it happens. But they're fun people to create onscreen. They're like hippy mountain men. They're not hippies, per se; it's this mountain man kind of mystical person. That I did not grow up with in Dade County! We don't have mystical mountain men in Miami.

Q: Do you think of your characters as unlikable?

A: No, I think of them as really imperfect. But I don't worry about them being likable. I have empathy for them and I don't think I've made a movie with anyone that I couldn't relate to on some level. Like, I didn't really relate to Meek, but I related to what it was like being stuck under a Meek. I related to how other people had deal with Meek. I guess the preacher in *Meek* was probably the hardest leap for me, to relate to someone who's really steeped in faith. He is a God-fearing person, and is motivated by it to press on; if he'll sacrifice a certain amount, he thinks that God will basically come through for him. With *Old Joy*, I felt like I really related to the worst qualities in Kurt. Because I related to that, I also wanted there to be other qualities that you see—people are just a mixed bag, and there's selfishness, and there's protectiveness, and there's manipulativeness, and friendship. I'm not out of my way to make sure someone's likable. I want them to be interesting. You know, Museum of the Moving Image had a forum on *Wendy and Lucy*, and overall, in Q&As and [other feedback], there was a lot of "Wendy gets what she deserves. She makes a lot of bad decisions."

Q: [Katherine Fusco:] Her students have had that response. [Nicole Seymour:] Yeah, often their reactions are the same as that supermarket clerk character: "She shouldn't have had a dog! She can't afford it." And I'm like "What is wrong with you monsters?!" [Laughter.]

A: I think it's a class issue. I mean, don't you watch *Teen Mom*?? The bad decisions never stop coming! [Laughter.] But I empathize with those girls. Like, "Here comes another bad decision! It's gonna last forever! Oh, you're seventeen and you have twins and you're gonna get pregnant again? With a new boyfriend? Good idea!" I don't hate them for their bad decisions, and I didn't hate Wendy for her bad decisions, and it was more just a question of "Yeah, there's going to be some bad decision making going on."

Q: "Let's watch it!"

A: Though, you know, I was just listening to the radio the other morning, and there was the argument against fracking, and for fracking, in New York, and one woman who has ten kids and lives upstate is like "We have all these Hollywood actors coming in telling us not to frack. And I need the money to frack!" And of course in my mind, I'm like "So, we all have to live with fracking so you can have ten kids?" It's not like I don't have judgments about people. I'm super judgmental! But with my characters, like the character in *Night Moves* that Jesse Eisenberg plays, it's interesting to have someone be outside people's comfort zone enough that you wonder if you can stir some empathy in them. And I bet—am betting—that I can—I was gonna say, I'm betting that I can get more empathy for someone who does something really radical that can harm people, who's a man, who fucks up in *Night Moves* than you could get for Wendy for stealing a can of dog food, or not making a good decision about how she spends her money. I mean, look back at those early Jack Nicholson films; he's such an asshole, but a charismatic one, right? Everybody loves him! I don't know that there's the same amount of leniency for Wendy. . . . I was amazed at how much people were mad at Wendy. She probably represents what a lot of people think of as the welfare state.

Q: You've already told us about your unshakable narrative habit, but we'd like to hear a bit more about your visual style. When you're working, how much are you thinking about crafting images versus telling a story?

A: It's just all wrapped in there. I'm not in a bird's-eye view, super analytical about everything. I am in the fact of just spending months in that desert saying, does this space work for this moment in the story? Where's the right space for this surprise, or this, or how does the landscape help either reinforce the story or offer some kind of subtext to or counter to, how's the landscape playing in in those ways? They're all questions that get answered by being inside exactly what we're doing. I'm not thinking of them in some bigger way, just in the immediacy of what this story means.

Q: Do you see *Night Moves* as continuing certain elements or themes that you've worked on before? You've mentioned that it's a thriller.

A: Well, I sort of think of *Old Joy* and *Wendy and Lucy* and *Meek's* as—we've talked about them in terms of a trilogy; it just always felt that way. This feels different than those films. I think it's less observational and it's a bit more subjective; you're more in it. And it has more plot; it has more music than some of the films have recently had. . . . Even editing it was just such a different experience. It wasn't like "This could be put together in lots of different ways." The story kept dictating what I was allowed to use, and what I wasn't allowed to use, and any extra moments would throw things off track. So, it's different in those ways. I mean, in *Meek's* we're in it with the characters and we know what they're after and what's in their way, and I guess that's true for *Wendy and Lucy*. But *Night Moves* is a little more pressing. But it still has quiet and stuff like that. But it's still a very process-oriented film, like, the process of getting–doing something. It's hard to think, "it's not finished yet!"

Q: What are your future projects?

A: Oh, I don't have any. Isn't that frightening? Right now *Night Moves* is pretty all-consuming. But, usually, there's another vine to jump to. So after *Night Moves*, either it will feel like "open space, relaxing" or be a total panic, like "your life is nothing without a project!" I don't know. Stay tuned!

Q: Well, thank you so much. This was fun.

A: Thanks for coming out here; I really appreciate it. You came such a long way. You should go do something in Queens!

Filmography

River of Grass (1994)
USA
Production: Good Machine
Distribution: Strand Releasing
Producer: Jesse Hartman
Associate Producers: Larry Fessenden and Susan A. Stover
Director: Kelly Reichardt
Screenplay: Kelly Reichardt (from a story by Jesse Hartman and Reichardt)
Cinematography: Jim Denault
Editor: Larry Fessenden
Music: John Hill
Costumes: Sara Jane Slotnick
Principal Cast: Lisa Bowman (Cozy Ryder), Larry Fessenden (Lee Ray Harold), Dick Russell (Jimmy Ryder)
Format: 35 mm, color
100 min.

Ode (1999)
USA
Production: Glass Eye Pix
Producer: Susan A. Stover
Assistant Production Manager: T. Colin Dodd
Director: Kelly Reichardt
Screenplay: Kelly Reichardt (based on the novel by Herman Raucher)
Cinematography: Kelly Reichardt
Editor: Philip Harrison
Music: Will Oldham, Paul Oldham, and Yo La Tengo
Art Direction: Todd Haynes
Sound: Susan A. Stover
Sound Edit and Mix: Nicholas Montgomery

Principal Cast: Kevin Poole (Billy Joe McAllister), Heather Gottlieb (Bobbie Lee Hartley), Jon Wurster (James), Bonnie Johnson (Mrs. Hartley)
Format: 8mm, color
48 min.

Then, a Year (2001)
USA
Production Company: Glasseye Pix
Director: Kelly Reichardt
Dialogue Editor: Larry Wineland
Music: Pamelia Kurstin
Editor: Kelly Reichardt
Sound Mixer: Jesse Ehredt
Format: 8mm, color
14 min.

Travis (2004)
USA
Director: Kelly Reichardt
Editor: Kelly Reichardt
Assistant Editor: Mike Olenick
Music: Ira Kaplan
Sound Mixer: Paul Hill
Format: Color
11 min.

Old Joy (2006)
USA
Production: Film Science, Van Hoy/Knudsen, Washington Square Films
Distribution: Kino International
Executive Producers: Joshua Blum, Todd Haynes, Mike S. Ryan, Rajen Savjani
Producers: Lars Knudsen, Neil Kopp, Anish Savjani, Jay Van Hoy
Senior Postproduction Producer: Julie Fischer
Director: Kelly Reichardt
Screenplay: Jonathan Raymond and Kelly Reichardt (based on Raymond's short story "Train Choir")
Cinematography: Peter Sillen
Editor: Kelly Reichardt
Music: Yo La Tengo and Smokey Hormel
Sound Design: Daniel Perlin
Principal Cast: Daniel London (Mark), Will Oldham (Kurt), Tanya Smith (Tanya, Mark's wife), Lucy the Dog (Lucy), Darren Prolsen (homeless man)
Format: 16 mm, color
76 min.

Wendy and Lucy (2008)
USA
Production: Field Guide Films, Film Science, Glass Eye Pix, Washington Square Films
Distribution: Oscilloscope Laboratories
Executive Producers: Joshua Blum, Todd Haynes, Phil Morrison, Rajen Savjani
Producers: Larry Fessenden, Neil Kopp, Anish Savjani
Director: Kelly Reichardt
Screenplay: Jonathan Raymond and Kelly Reichardt
Cinematography: Sam Levy
Editor: Kelly Reichardt
Music: Smokey Hormel and Will Oldham
Sound Design: Eric Offin and Leslie Shatz
Costumes: Amanda Needham
Production Design: Ryan Smith
Principal Cast: Michelle Williams (Wendy), Lucy the Dog (Lucy), Will Oldham (Icky), Walter Dalton (security guard), John Robinson (Andy the stock boy), Ayanna Berkshire (pound employee), Will Patton (mechanic)
Format: 16mm, color
80 min.

Meek's Cutoff (2010)
USA
Production Company: Evenstar Films, Film Science, Harmony Productions, Primitive Nerd
Distribution: Oscilloscope Laboratories
Executive Producers: Todd Haynes, Phil Morrison, Andrew Pope, Laura Rosenthal, Mike S. Ryan, Rajen Savjani, Steven Tuttleman
Producers: Elizabeth Cuthrell, Neil Kopp, Anish Savjani, David Urrutia
Coproducer: Vincent Savino
Director: Kelly Reichardt
Screenplay: Jonathan Raymond
Cinematography: Christopher Blauvelt
Editor: Kelly Reichardt
Music: Jeff Grace
Sound Design: Leslie Shatz
Art Direction: Kat Uhlmansiek
Costumes: Victoria Farrell
Principal Cast: Michelle Williams (Emily Tetherow), Will Patton (Solomon Tetherow), Bruce Greenwood (Stephen Meek), Zoe Kazan (Millie Gately), Paul Dano (Thomas Gately), Shirley Henderson (Glory White), Neal Huff (William White), Tommy Nelson (Jimmy White), Rod Rondeaux (The Indian)

Format: 35 mm, color
104 min.

Night Moves (2013)
USA
Production: Maybach Film Productions, Film Science, Tipping Point Productions, RT Features
Distribution: Cinedigm
Executive Producers: Alejandro De Leon, Larry Fessenden, Todd Haynes, Saerom Kim, Lourenco Sant'Anna
Producers: Saemi Kim, Neil Kopp, Chris Maybach, Anish Savjani, Rodrigo Teixeira
Coproducer: Vincent Savino
Associate Producer: Roxane Mesquida
Director: Kelly Reichardt
Screenplay: Jonathan Raymond and Kelly Reichardt
Cinematography: Christopher Blauvelt
Editor: Kelly Reichardt
Music: Jeff Grace
Sound Design: Kent Sparling
Production Design: Elliott Hostetter
Art Director: Almitra Corey
Costumes: Victoria Farrell
Principal Cast: Dakota Fanning (Dena Brauer), Jesse Eisenberg (Josh Stamos), Peter Sarsgaard (Harmon)
Format: Color
112 min.

Certain Women (2016)
USA
Production: Film Science, Stage 6 Films
Distribution: LFR Films, Park Circus, Peripher, IFC Films, Sony Pictures Worldwide Acquisitions
Executive Producers: Larry Fessenden, Todd Haynes, Nathan Kelly
Producers: Neil Kopp, Vincent Savino, Anish Savjani
Director: Kelly Reichardt
Screenplay: Kelly Reichardt, based on stories by Maile Meloy
Cinematography: Christopher Blauvelt
Editor: Kelly Reichardt
Music: Jeff Grace
Production Design: Anthony Gasparro
Costumes: April Napier

Principal Cast: Laura Dern (Laura), Lily Gladstone (The Rancher), Jared Harris (Fuller), James Le Gros (Ryan), Kristen Stewart (Elizabeth Travis), Michelle Williams (Gina)
Format: 16mm, color
107 min.

Bibliography

Adams, Sam. "Kelly Reichardt and Jon Raymond." *A.V. Club*, April 26, 2011. http://www.avclub.com/article/kelly-reichardt-and-jon-raymond-55095.

Bad Day at Black Rock. Directed by John Sturges. MGM, 1955.

Bal [*Honey*]. Directed by Semih Kaplanoğlu. Kaplan Film, 2010.

Baur, John I. H. *The Inlander: The Life and Work of Charles Burchfield, 1893–1967*. Newark: University of Delaware Press, 1982.

Bazin, André. "Bicycle Thieves." In *André Bazin and Italian Neorealism*, edited by Bert Cardullo, 61–73. New York: Continuum International, 2011.

———. "Cinematic Realism and the Italian School of Liberation." In *André Bazin and Italian Neorealism*, edited by Bert Cardullo, 29–50. New York: Continuum International, 2011.

———. "De Sica: Metteur en Scène." *What Is Cinema?* 2 vols. Selected and translated by Hugh Gray, 2:61–78. Berkeley: University of California Press, 2005.

Berger, John. "Millet and the Peasant." In *About Looking*, 69–78. New York: Pantheon, 1980.

Berlant, Lauren. *Cruel Optimism*. Durham, NC: Duke University Press, 2011.

Bordwell, David. "The Art Cinema as a Mode of Film Practice." In *Film Theory and Criticism: Introductory Readings*, edited by Leo Braudy and Marshall Cohen, 716–24. New York: Oxford University Press, 1999.

———. n.d. "Measurement Theory." *Cinemetrics*. http://www.cinemetrics.lv/bordwell.php.

Brady, Tara. "Kelly Reichardt: Cinema's Slow Hand Lights the Fuse." *Irish Times*, August 24, 2014. http://www.irishtimes.com/culture/film/kelly-reichardt-cinema-s-slow-hand-lights-the-fuse-1.1910794.

Buscombe, Ed, and Graham Fuller. "The Oregon Trail." *Sight and Sound* 21, no. 5 (2011): 38–42.

Colford, Caitlin. "An Interview with Jon Raymond." *The Rumpus*, April 29, 2011. http://therumpus.net/2011/04/an-interview-with-jon-raymond/.

Dan. "Full Time RV Travel—Quick Overnight Stays. . . . What Do You Do?" *Ready to Go Fulltime RVing* [blog], September 2009. http://readytogofulltimerving.blogspot.com/2012/09/full-time-rv-travelquick-overnight.html.

Dawn, Karen. "Best Friends Need Shelter, Too." *Washington Post*, September 10, 2005. http://www.washingtonpost.com/wp-dyn/content/article/2005/09/09/AR2005090901824.html.

Del Savio, Lorenzo, and Matteo Mameli. "The Evaporation of Democracy." *Truthout*, October 20, 2014. http://www.truth-out.org/opinion/item/26879.

De Luca, Tiago, and Nuno Barradas Jorge, eds. *Slow Movies*. Edinburgh: Edinburgh University Press, 2016.

Devroy, Ann. "Upbeat Bush Steps Up Rhetoric." *Washington Post*, October 30, 1992. http://tech.mit.edu/V112/N53/bush.53w.html.

Easy Rider. Directed by Dennis Hopper. Colombia Pictures, 1969.

Ehrenreich, Barbara. *Fear of Falling: The Inner Life of the Middle Class*. New York: Harper Collins, 1990.

———. *Nickel and Dimed: On (Not) Getting By in America*. New York: Henry Holt, 2001.

Everett, Wendy. "Lost in Transition? The European Road Movie, or a Genre 'Adrift in the Cosmos.'" *Literature-Film Quarterly* 37, no. 3 (2009): 165–75.

Fay, Jennifer. "Seeing/Loving Animals: André Bazin's Posthumanism." *Journal of Visual Culture* 7, no. 1 (2008): 41–64.

Five Easy Pieces. Directed by Bob Rafelson. Columbia Pictures, 1975.

Flanagan, Matthew. "Towards an Aesthetic of Slow in Contemporary Cinema." *16:9* 6, no. 29 (November 2008). http://www.16-9.dk/2008-11/side11_inenglish.htm.

Foster, Mary. "Evacuation of Pets a Priority after Katrina." *Huffington Post*. Associated Press, August 24, 2010. http://www.huffingtonpost.com/huff-wires/20100824/us-katrina-snowball-s-lesson/.

Gentry, Bobbie. "Ode to Billie Joe." *Ode to Billie Joe*. Capitol Records, 1967.

Goldenburg, Suzanne. "Why Global Water Shortages Pose Threat of Terror and War." *Guardian*, February 8, 2014. http://www.theguardian.com/environment/2014/feb/09/global-water-shortages-threat-terror-war.

Gorfinkel, Elena. "Exhausted Drift: Austerity, Dispossession and the Politics of Slow in Kelly Reichardt's *Meek's Cutoff*." In *Slow Cinema*, edited by Tiago de Luca and Nuno Barradas Jorge, 123–36. Edinburgh: Edinburgh University Press, 2016.

———. "Weariness, Waiting: Enduration and Art Cinema's Tired Bodies." *Discourse* 34, no. 2 (2012): 311–47.

Greenpeace. "Where Does E-waste End Up?" February 24, 2009. http://www.greenpeace.org/international/en/campaigns/detox/electronics/the-e-waste-problem/where-does-e-waste-end-up/.

Gross, Terry. "Going West: The Making of *Meek's Cutoff*." Kelly Reichardt interview. *Fresh Air*, April 14, 2011.

Guthmann, Edward. "A Man Faces His 'Eternity' and His Past." *San Francisco Chronicle*, September 10, 1999. http://www.sfgate.com/movies/article/A-Man-Faces-His-Eternity-and-His-Past-2909205.php.

Haraway, Donna. *The Companion Species Manifesto: Dogs, People, and Significant Otherness*. Chicago: Prickly Paradigm, 2003.

Harrison, Sarah K. *Waste Matters: Urban Margins in Contemporary Literature*. New York: Routledge, 2016.

Holden, Stephen. "Just Too Bored to Be Bad." Review. *New York Times*, August 4, 1995. http://www.nytimes.com/1995/08/04/movies/film-review-just-too-bored-to-be-bad.html.

Honig, Bonnie. *Emergency Politics: Paradox, Law, Democracy*. Princeton, NJ: Princeton University Press, 2011.

Hornaday, Ann. "Director Kelly Reichardt on *Meek's Cutoff* and Making Movies Her Way." *Washington Post*, May 20, 2011. http://www.washingtonpost.com/lifestyle/style/director-kelly-reichardt-on-meeks-cutoff-and-making-movies-her-way/2011/05/08/AFOloK7G_story.html.

Ingram, David. *Green Screen: Environmentalism and Hollywood Cinema*. Exeter, UK: University of Exeter Press, 2004.

Jaffe, Ira. *Slow Movies: Countering the Cinema of Action*. New York: Columbia University Press, 2014.

James, Nick. "Passive Aggressive." *Sight and Sound* 20, no. 4 (April 2010): 5.

John and Amy. "Comment about Wal-Mart 'Camping.'" April 21, 2006. http://www.barthmobile.com/eve/forums/a/tpc/f/9331087061/m/6031094771.

Kara, Selmin. "Anthropocinema: Cinema in the Age of Mass Extinctions." In *Post-Cinema: Theorizing 21st Century Film*, edited by Shane Denson and Julia Leyda, n.p. Falmer, UK: Reframe, 2016. http://reframe.sussex.ac.uk/post-cinema/.

Kendall, Tina. "Staying on, or Getting off (the Bus): Approaching Speed in Cinema and Media Studies." *Cinema Journal* 55, no. 2 (2016): 112–18.

Kierkegaard, Søren. "*Either/Or, a Fragment of Life, I*." In *Essential Kierkegaard*, edited by Howard and Edna Hong, 37–65. Princeton, NJ: Princeton University Press, 2000.

King, Geoff. *Indiewood, USA: Where Hollywood Meets Independent Cinema*. London: I. B. Taurus, 2009.

Kitses, Jim. *Horizons West: Directing the Western from John Ford to Clint Eastwood*. London: British Film Institute, 2008.

Koepnick, Lutz. *On Slowness: Toward an Aesthetic of the Contemporary*. New York: Columbia University Press, 2014.

Kois, Dan. "Eating Your Cultural Vegetables." *New York Times*, April 29, 2011. http://www.nytimes.com/2011/05/01/magazine/mag-01Riff-t.html?pagewanted=all&_r=0.

LaSalle, Mick. "Ecoterrorism from an Odd Angle." *San Francisco Chronicle*, June 5, 2014. http://www.sfgate.com/movies/article/Night-Moves-review-Ecoterrorism-from-an-odd-5531354.php.

Lattimer, James. "Beyond Neo-Neo Realism: Reconfigurations of Neorealist Narration in Kelly Reichardt's *Meek's Cutoff*." *Cinephile* 7, no. 2 (2011): 37–41.

Longworth, Karina. "Going the Distance with *Meek's Cutoff* Director Kelly Reichardt." *Village Voice*, April 6, 2011. http://www.villagevoice.com/2011-04-06/film/going-the-distance-with-meek-s-cutoff-director-kelly-reichardt/.

Lukács, Georg. *The Historical Novel*. Translated by Hannah and Stanley Mitchell. London: Merlin, 1962.

MacDonald, Scott. "Toward an Eco-Cinema." *ISLE: Interdisciplinary Studies in Literature and Environment* 11, no. 2 (2004): 107–32.

Manhatta. Directed by Charles Sheeler and Paul Strand. 1921.

Mazel, David. "Annie Dillard and the Book of Job: Notes toward a Postnatural Ecocriticism." In *Coming into Contact: Explorations in Ecocritical Theory and Practice*, edited by Annie Merrill Ingram, Ian Marshall, Daniel J. Philippon, and Adam W. Sweeting. Athens: University of Georgia Press, 2007.

McClanahan, Erik. "The Movies That Changed My Life: Kelly Reichardt, Director of *Night Moves*." *Playlist*, May 28, 2014. http://blogs.indiewire.com/theplaylist/my-life-in-film-kelly-reichardt-director-of-night-moves-20140524.

Night Moves. Directed by Arthur Penn. Warner, 1975.

Nixon, Rob. *Slow Violence and the Environmentalism of the Poor*. Cambridge, MA: Harvard University Press, 2011.

Pennies from Heaven. Directed by Herbert Ross. MGM, 1981.

Perren, Alisa. *Indie, Inc.: Miramax and the Transformation of Hollywood in the 1990s*. Austin: University of Texas Press, 2013.

Perry, Douglas. "Writer Jon Raymond Sees His Work Realized in Oregon Films." *Oregonian/Oregon Live*, January 5, 2009. http://www.oregonlive.com/movies/2009/01/writer_jon_raymond_sees_his_wo.html.

Raban, Jonathan. "Metronaturals." *Driving Home: An American Journey*, 462–70. New York: Pantheon Books, 2010.

Raymond, Jonathan. Personal communication with the authors. March 10, 2015. E-mail.

———. "Old Joy." In *Livability: Stories*, 1–21. New York: Bloomsbury, 2008.

———. "Train Choir." In *Livability: Stories*, 206–60. New York: Bloomsbury, 2008.

Reichardt, Kelly. Interviewed by Katherine Fusco and Nicole Seymour. March 27, 2013.

———. Interviewed by Todd Haynes. *BOMB* 53 (Fall 1995). http://bombmagazine.org/article/1891/kelly-reichardt.

———. Interviewed by Gus Van Sant. *BOMB* 105 (Fall 2008). http://bombsite.com/issues/105/articles/3182.

Romney, Jonathan. "In Search of Lost Time." *Sight and Sound* 20, no. 2 (2010): 43.

Rowin, Michael Joshua. "Q&A: Kelly Reichardt, Director of *Old Joy*." *Stop Smiling*, September 22, 2006. http://stopsmilingonline.com/story_print.php?id=655.

Salvato, Nick. *Obstruction*. Durham, NC: Duke University Press, 2016.

Schoonover, Karl. "Wastrels of Time: Slow Cinema's Laboring Body, the Political Spectator, and the Queer." *Framework* 53, no. 1 (Spring 2012): 65–78.

Scott, A. O. "Neo-Neorealism." *New York Times*, March 17, 2009. http://www.nytimes.com/2009/03/22/magazine/22neorealism-t.html?pagewanted=all&_r=0.

Seymour, Nicole. "Down with People: Queer Tendencies and Troubling Racial Politics in Antinatalist Discourse." In *International Perspectives in Feminist Ecocriticism*, edited by Simon Estok, Greta Gaard, and Serpil Oppermann. New York: Routledge, 2013.

———. *Strange Natures: Futurity, Empathy, and the Queer Ecological Imagination*. Champaign: University of Illinois Press, 2013.

Shampoo. Directed by Hal Ashby. Columbia, 1975.

Shaviro, Steven. "Slow Cinema vs Fast Films." *The Pinocchio Theory*, May 12, 2010. http://www.shaviro.com/Blog/?p=891.

Singer, Ben. "*Jeanne Dielman*: Cinematic Interrogation and 'Amplification.'" *Millennium Film Journal* 22 (Winter 1989/Spring 1990): 56–75.

Standing, Guy. *The Precariat: The New Dangerous Class*. London: Bloomsbury Academic, 2011.

Sternfeld, Joel. *On This Site: Landscape in Memoriam*. San Francisco: Chronicle, 1997.

Stevens, Dana. "Meek's Cutoff." *Slate*, April 8, 2011. http://www.slate.com/articles/arts/movies/2011/04/meeks_cutoff.html.

Stewart, Ryan. "Redefining Success: An Interview with Kelly Reichardt." *Slant Magazine*, December 5, 2008. http://www.slantmagazine.com/film/feature/redefining-success-an-interview-with-kelly-reichardt/44.

Sumner, David Thomas, and Lisa Weidman. "Eco-terrorism or Eco-tage: An Argument for the Proper Frame." *Interdisciplinary Studies in Literature and Environment* 20, no. 3 (2013): 1–22.

Svendson, Lars. *A Philosophy of Boredom*. London: Reaktion, 2005.

Thelma and Louise. Directed by Ridley Scott. Pathé, 1991.

Thomas, Kevin. "*River*: Fresh Sendup of Lovers on the Lam." *Los Angeles Times*, October 13, 1995. http://articles.latimes.com/1995–10–13/entertainment/ca-56450_1_kelly-reichardt.

Tuttle, Harry. "Slow Films, Easy Life (Sight and Sound)." *Unspoken Cinema*, May 12, 2010. http://unspokencinema.blogspot.com/2010/05/slow-films-easy-life-sight.html.

Uncle Boonmee Who Can Recall His Past Lives. Directed by Apichatpong Weerasethakul. Kick the Machine, 2011.

United States Defense Intelligence Agency. *Global Water Security*. Intelligence Community Assessment. Washington, DC: Government Printing Office, 2012. http://www.dni.gov/files/documents/Special%20Report_ICA%20Global%20Water%20Security.pdf.

Weisman, Alan. *The World without Us*. New York: Thomas Dunne, 2007.

Wherezitat? Locate-a-Walmart. Boulder City, NV: Wherezitat, 2009.
Winter, Elisa. "Filmmaker Kelly Reichardt, *Wendy and Lucy*." *Gothamist*, December 8, 2008. http://gothamist.com/2008/12/08/filmmaker_kelly_reichardt_wendy_and.php.
Wright, Will. *Six Guns and Society: A Structural Study of the Western*. Berkeley: University of California Press, 1975.

Index

Katherine Fusco is an assistant professor of English at the University of Nevada, Reno. She is the author of *Silent Film and U.S. Naturalist Literature: Time, Narrative, and Modernity*.

Nicole Seymour is an assistant professor of English at California State University, Fullerton. She is the author of *Strange Natures: Futurity, Empathy, and the Queer Ecological Imagination*.

Books in the series Contemporary Film Directors

Nelson Pereira dos Santos
Darlene J. Sadlier

Abbas Kiarostami
Mehrnaz Saeed-Vafa and Jonathan Rosenbaum

Joel and Ethan Coen
R. Barton Palmer

Claire Denis
Judith Mayne

Wong Kar-wai
Peter Brunette

Edward Yang
John Anderson

Pedro Almodóvar
Marvin D'Lugo

Chris Marker
Nora Alter

Abel Ferrara
Nicole Brenez, translated by Adrian Martin

Jane Campion
Kathleen McHugh

Jim Jarmusch
Juan Suárez

Roman Polanski
James Morrison

Manoel de Oliveira
John Randal Johnson

Neil Jordan
Maria Pramaggiore

Paul Schrader
George Kouvaros

Jean-Pierre Jeunet
Elizabeth Ezra

Terrence Malick
Lloyd Michaels

Sally Potter
Catherine Fowler

Atom Egoyan
Emma Wilson

Albert Maysles
Joe McElhaney

Jerry Lewis
Chris Fujiwara

Jean-Pierre and Luc Dardenne
Joseph Mai

Michael Haneke
Peter Brunette

Alejandro González Iñárritu
Celestino Deleyto and Maria del Mar Azcona

Lars von Trier
Linda Badley

Hal Hartley
Mark L. Berrettini

François Ozon
Thibaut Schilt

Steven Soderbergh
Aaron Baker

Mike Leigh
Sean O'Sullivan

D.A. Pennebaker
Keith Beattie

Jacques Rivette
Mary M. Wiles

Kim Ki-duk
Hye Seung Chung

Philip Kaufman
Annette Insdorf

Richard Linklater
David T. Johnson

David Lynch
Justus Nieland

John Sayles
David R. Shumway

Dario Argento
L. Andrew Cooper

Todd Haynes
Rob White

Christian Petzold
Jaimey Fisher

Spike Lee
Todd McGowan

Terence Davies
Michael Koresky

Francis Ford Coppola
Jeff Menne

Emir Kusturica
Giorgio Bertellini

Agnès Varda
Kelley Conway

John Lasseter
Richard Neupert

Paul Thomas Anderson
George Toles

Cristi Puiu
Monica Filimon

Wes Anderson
Donna Kornhaber

Jan Švankmajer
Keith Leslie Johnson

Kelly Reichardt
Katherine Fusco
and Nicole Seymour

The University of Illinois Press
is a founding member of the
Association of American University Presses.

University of Illinois Press
1325 South Oak Street
Champaign, IL 61820-6903
www.press.uillinois.edu